DARRELL D GENZLINGER

ONE NEW MAN

JESUS CHRIST IS COMING VERY VERY SOON!

WestBow
PRESS
A DIVISION OF THOMAS NELSON

WestBow Press books may be ordered through booksellers or by contacting:

WestBow Press
A Division of Thomas Nelson
1663 Liberty Drive
Bloomington, IN 47403
www.westbowpress.com
1-(866) 928-1240

Because of the dynamic nature of the Internet, any web addresses or links contained in this book may have changed since publication and may no longer be valid. The views expressed in this work are solely those of the author and do not necessarily reflect the views of the publisher, and the publisher hereby disclaims any responsibility for them.

Any people depicted in stock imagery provided by Thinkstock are models, and such images are being used for illustrative purposes only.

Certain stock imagery © Thinkstock.

ISBN: 978-1-4497-3874-7 (sc)

Library of Congress Control Number: 2012901743

Printed in the United States of America

WestBow Press rev. date: 04/17/2012

INTRODUCTION

Hello,

I am a Christian. My purpose for writing this book is to share the love of Jesus Christ with those who don't know Him, and to assist those who desire to know Him better.

I believe we are in the End Time. The Holy Bible is the Word of God, and it has much to say about the Lord's Second Coming. About one-third of the Bible deals with prophecy; some has already been fulfilled, but a lot of it

has yet to be fulfilled.

While we wait for the Lord to return what better way to pass the time than to read, to study, and to share the Word of God with others, and to pray for His quick return.

If you have a question or comment please send me an e-mail.

ONE NEW MAN is a composite of many articles on my website http://.wwwdarrellgenzlinger.com written over the last nineteen years. This book was originally written in 2011.

Darrell Genzlinger: darrellgenzlinger@gmail.com

Dedication

Dedication

I dedicate this book to my lovely wife, Betty, of 60 years and to our four wonderful children Douglas, Curtis, Debra, and Tamra.

CONTENTS

Introduction v

Dedication vi

Chapter 1:   Frequently Asked Questions 1

Chapter 2:   My Reasons for Believing We are in the End Times 4

Chapter 3:   History of the Doctrine on the Millennial Reign 6

Chapter 4:   A Lutheran's View on Eschatology 19

Chapter 5:   On the Road to the 7th Millennium 25

Chapter 6:   Critique on Africanus' Chronology 34

Chapter 7:   Dating Christ's Death and Resurrection 40

Chapter 8:   An Understanding of Eschatology 52

Chapter 9:   Passages Supporting a 6000-Year Earth and a Millennial Reign of Christ 56

Chapter 10: Definition of Terms Dealing with End Time Events 60

Chapter 11: Thought Provoking Questions About The Bible 62

Chapter 12: Recovering the Remnant of Israel for the Second Time 68

Chapter 13: References to 'The Day' 70

Chapter 14: Israel's Third Temple 73

Chapter 15: The 70th Year of Jubilee 76

Chapter 16: The Study of Revelation 83

Chapter 17: Conclusions 109

Notes and Comments 110

CHAPTER 1
FREQUENTLY ASKED QUESTIONS

1. Do you know for certain that if you were to die today you would go to heaven?

   O   Yes
   O   No
   O   I don't know

If your answer is not a resounding and confident 'Yes' to that question, you probably should read on.

2. Do you think that you deserve heaven?

   O   Yes
   O   No
   O   I don't know

If your answer is not a resounding and confident 'No' to that question, you probably should read on.

3. Have you ever committed any sin or sins in your life?

   O   Yes
   O   No
   O   I don't know

If your answer is not a resounding and confident 'Yes' to that question, you should read what the Bible has to say in Romans 3:23. **"For all have sinned and fall short of the glory of God."** (NKJV)*

4. Does God require you to be sinless to get into his heaven?

Yes, and again I say Yes. God requires you to be sinless. God says in Ezekiel 18:4, **"The soul who sins shall die"** and again in Matthew 5:48, **"Therefore you shall be perfect, just as your Father in heaven is perfect."**

That is an impossible requirement since you and I are already sinners. We know that all have sinned because all have died in the past, or are going to die in the future. Even those who are yet to be born. We are doomed to go to hell.

5. Who is God, or rather what are some <u>attributes of God</u>?

He is all-powerful. He created the world and everything in it by just speaking.
He is all-knowing. He knows all of the past, present, and future about everything.
He is all-present. He is everywhere all the time.
He is just, holy, righteous. A just God—Isaiah 45:21; God is holy—Leviticus 11:44; The Lord is righteous—Zephaniah 3:5
He is merciful, gracious, loving. The Lord being merciful—Genesis 19:16 & Exodus 34:6; God is love—I John 4:16.

6. Will God let human sinners into heaven?

Yes and No. Yes, if you have the correct credentials. No, if you don't.

7. What are the correct credentials?

"He who believes and is baptized will be saved; but he who does not believe will be condemned." Mark 16:16.

8. What must we believe?

Believe in God's Son, Jesus the Christ.

God tells us in <u>John 3:16</u>. **"For God so loved the world that He gave His <u>only begotten Son</u>, that whoever believes in Him should not perish, but have everlasting life."** And again, God says in Luke 9:35, **"This is My beloved Son. Hear Him!"**

9. Who is Jesus?

The beloved Son of God—but He is much more. Jesus is God (John 1:1 & 1:14 and John 10:30.)

Job was complaining about his lot in life. **"For God is not a man, as I am, that I may answer Him, and that we should go to court together. Nor is there any mediator between us, who may lay his hand on us both."** Job 9:32-33. But Job was wrong.

Jesus is the Man. The God Man. He is the Mediator between God and man. He is the Seed promised to Adam and Eve after they fell into sin (Genesis 3:15). He is the Prophet promised to Moses after the Exodus (Deuteronomy 18:15). He is the King promised to David that would reign forever (II Samuel 7:12). He is the Good Teacher from God (John 3:2).

Jesus Christ lived the perfect, sinless life that we couldn't. He died on the cross for our sins by crucifixion and was buried. After three days he rose again to defeat sin, death, and the devil for us.

10. So, what does heaven cost me?

Nothing. That's right. Nothing. Zilch. Heaven is a free gift.

You can not work your way into heaven otherwise it wouldn't be free.

God offers us the free gift of heaven to whosoever believes in Jesus. **"For by grace you have been saved through faith, and that not of yourselves; it is the gift of God, not of works, lest anyone should boast."** Ephesians 2:8-9. And in Romans 6:23 He puts it this way, **"For the wages of sin is death, but the gift of God is eternal life in Christ Jesus our Lord."**

11. What is grace and faith?

Grace is simply defined by an acronym: **G**od's **R**iches **A**t **C**hrist's **E**xpense

Faith is the key that opens the door to heaven.

Faith is not merely an intellectual awareness of a historical fact. For example, a certain man called Jesus lived 2000 years ago. The Bible teaches us that even the devil believes in Christ in this way and he shutters. But that won't do. Nor is it temporal faith. Some people trust in Christ for temporal things of life, such as good health, or their children's well-being, or their finances, or strength, or guidance—the things that have to do only with this life that we live right here.

Faith is trusting Jesus Christ alone for salvation. Jesus is the Savior of our souls.

12. Where do we get this faith?

From Jesus. Pray to Jesus for faith to believe. Just ask Jesus to forgive your sins, all those sins that you have ever committed and even those sins that you don't remember, and invite Jesus to come into your life and to be your teacher and the Lord of your life. The words aren't so important but that they come from the heart. I have copied a prayer for this occasion.

Lord Jesus, I want you to come in and take over my life right now. I am a sinner. I have been trusting in myself and my own good works. But now I place my trust in you. I accept you as my own personal Savior. I believe you died for me. I receive you as Lord and Master of my life. Help me to turn from my sins and to follow you. I accept the free gift of eternal life. I am not worthy of it but I thank you for it. Amen.

If you prayed this prayer and meant it then read John 6:47.

Now, how would you answer the first three questions on this web page?

* If you don't have a Bible you can get a copy of the King James Version on-line from <http://etext.lib.virginia.edu/kjv.browse.html>. I have used the New King James Version here. There is little difference between the KJV and the NKJV except the KJV uses some archaic language.

CHAPTER 2
MY REASONS FOR BELIEVING WE ARE IN THE END TIMES

1. Jews are returning to their land for the second time—Isa. 11:11.

2. Nuclear, chemical & biological weapons of mass destruction exist to contaminate areas for 40 years—Ez. 29:11 & Rev. 8:10-11.

3. Israel has become a "Garden of Eden"—Ez. 36:32-35.

   a. Through irrigation Israel gets three crops a year. 'Plowers will overtake reapers'—Amos 9:13.
   b. Trees in great abundance; cedar, acacia, myrtle, oil, cypress, pine, fir, box trees—Isa. 41:19-20.

4. Rosh (Russia??), Persia (Iran), Ethiopia and Libya are allies and appear to be ready to take up arms against Israel—Ez. 38:5 & 8.

5. We are in the last <u>world empire</u>, i.e., the revived Roman Empire, (feet of iron and clay) before the Stone (Jesus) grinds up the world empires—Dan. 2:27-45.

6. Israel is planning for

   a. re-establishing animal sacrifices—Dan. 9:27,
   b. and rebuilding the temple—Amos 9:11.

7. Knowledge has increased (1 calculation/sec in 1940 to 1 billion calculations/sec in 1992)—Dan. 12:4.

8. Many run to and fro (travel has increased from 40 mph in 1900 to 18,000 mph in 1992)—Dan. 12:4.

9. All nations (including the US) rising up against Israel—Zech. 12:3 & 14:2.

10. Events "prior to the end", in <u>Matthew 24</u>, have been fulfilled—

    a. wars and rumors of wars,
    b. nation against nation,
    c. kingdom against kingdom,
    d. increase in famines, pestilences (such as, AIDS), and earthquakes in various places,

    e.   many false christs and <u>false prophets</u> deceiving many,

    f.   gospel preached in all the world, particularly via geosynchronous satellites.

11. This generation has seen the fig tree (Israel) bud (become a nation)—Matt. 24:32-35.

    a.   Israel reborn in a day (May 15, 1948)—Isa. 66:8,

    b.   Israel shall be many days without a king, prince, or sacrifice & afterward they shall return—Hos. 3:4-5.

12. "Days of Noah" are being repeated (much sexual immorality and lawlessness)—Matt. 24:37-39.

13. Apostasy (great falling away) in society with New Age philosophy and in the churches with humanism—2 Thess. 2:3.

14. Approaching a cashless society—Rev. 13:17.

15. Knowing this first, that there shall come in the last days scoffers, walking after their own lusts—II Pet. 3:3.

16. About time for another cosmic event assuming approximate equal intervals in God's plan—

    a.   1656 years between creation and flood;

    b.   2348 years between flood and Christ's first coming (death and resurrection);

    c.   1959 years between Christ's death and resurrection and now.

17. "Six days of man" (6000 years) are about completed; the "Sabbath day" or "Lord's Day" is about here.

18. Fulfillment of prophecy for the last three of the seven Jewish Feast days, i.e., Rosh Hashanah, Day of Atonement, Feast of Tabernacles. If these Feast have a prophetic event associated with them there must be some people who would benefit from the prophecy. Is it the people who live during the seventh millennial period?

CHAPTER 3

HISTORY OF THE DOCTRINE ON THE MILLENNIAL REIGN

The authors and times of the writers on the subject of a messianic millennial reign of Jesus Christ on earth can be divided into two categories; those that were written <u>before the Christian era</u> began and those that were written after Christ walked on this earth.

I. <u>Before Christian Era</u>

Isaiah—720—700 B.C.
Ezekiel—585 B.C.
Zechariah—500 B.C.
<u>Septuagint</u> written between 285-246 B.C.
<u>Book of Jubilees</u> written between 109-105 B.C.

II. <u>Christian Era</u>

New Testament written—A.D. 50—100
The Revelation of Jesus Christ—written by the apostle John around A.D. 96
Epistle of Barnabas—written between A.D. 70 and 135
<u>Papias</u>—(A.D. c.70-c.155)
<u>Justin Martyr</u>—(A.D. c.110-c.165)
<u>Irenaeus</u>—(A.D. c.130-c.202)
Jews abandon Septuagint between A.D. 100-200
Christians abandon Septuagint between A.D. 500-1000

I. <u>Before Christian Era</u>

Early believers in the doctrine of the Messiah reigning on earth could have gotten its start with the inspired message proclaimed by the prophet Isaiah. In the latter part of the eighth century before the Christian era (c.740—700 B.C.) God told His people through the prophet Isaiah (Is. 65:17) that the Lord will create a new heavens and a new earth. **"For, behold, I create new heavens and a new earth: and the former shall not be remembered, nor come into mind."** Isaiah goes on to say in verse 20, **"There shall be no more thence an infant of days, nor an old man that hath not filled his days: for the child shall die an hundred years old; but the sinner being an hundred years old shall be accursed."** (KJV) Therefore, there is death in this new heavens and new earth prophesied in Isaiah 65. This is not eternal bliss which is what we claim heaven will be like. "... **and there shall be no more death, neither sorrow, nor crying; neither shall there be any more pain: for the former things are passed away."** (Rev. 21:4)

Then He prophesied in Isaiah 66:23, **"And it shall come to pass, that from one new moon to another, and from one sabbath to another, shall all flesh come to worship before me, saith the Lord."** It is interesting that Isaiah 66:23 uses the phrase 'before me'. As if the Messiah was standing (or sitting) there with all people coming to worship Him. We know the new heaven referred to in Isaiah 66:22-24 can not be the same heaven of eternal bliss which is described in the book of the Revelation of Jesus Christ. The heaven described in Rev. 21:22-25 has no sun or moon or night. Heaven will not need any sun or moon because it will be illuminated by the presence of God and His Lamb, Jesus Christ.

Prophecies in Ezekiel and Zechariah could also be interpreted by early Messianic believers to be fulfilled during the messianic reign. God spoke through Ezekiel during the sixth century pre-Christian era (c. 593—573 B.C.). Ezekiel 39:21 to 48:35 describes a yet to be instituted government. The government is a theocracy similar to that which was instituted for Israel at the time of Moses. The land will be divided equally among the 12 tribes of Israel. The temple and city are constructed in the midst of the property of the 12 tribes. The prophecy tells of a prince of Israel. This prince is not Jesus. Jesus is the King of kings and Lord of lords. The prince of Israel is given property adjacent to the holy district. The prince can give some of his own property to his sons as an inheritance. But if he gives some of his property to one of his servants it shall be returned in the year of liberty. (Ez. 46:16-17). The period called liberty or jubilee consists of seven Sabbath years or 49 years.

The nation of Israel will be celebrating New Moons, Sabbaths and Festivals with burnt offerings, grain offerings, and drink offerings as Israel did after they were instituted at Mt. Sinai.

Zechariah was God's spokesman during the latter part of the sixth century, in 520 to 518 B.C. or later. In Zechariah 13:2 the Lord says, **"And it shall come to pass in that day, saith the Lord of hosts, that I will cut off the names of the idols out of the land, and they shall no more be remembered."** What day do you think there will not be any idols? I think it will be the day that Jesus appears in person. Everyone will worship Him as Lord. There will be no Baal worship. No Asharoth worship. No Buddhism. No Hinduism. No Mohammedanism. No Mormonism. No astrological sign. No sports hero. No Wall Street wizard. I think, if for no other reason, when Christ comes in person to reign on earth, people will be ashamed to worship idols or even to acknowledge them.

The prophecy in Zechariah 14:19 tells of Egypt, and all nations, being punished for not keeping the Feast of Tabernacles. Again, the punishment given, or proposed, to Egypt would prevent this from being eternal bliss. I do believe that Egypt will be desolate for forty years. It will probably become desolate during the great tribulation. God foretells us through the prophet Ezekiel in chapter 29, verses 8-16, Egypt shall be uninhabited for a period of forty years where neither foot of man nor beast will pass through it.

Old testament prophecies in Isaiah, Ezekiel, and Zechariah would give the Jewish people ample reason for believing that the Messiah promised would set-up His kingdom here on earth.

The writings of Malachi closed out the canonized prophecies of the Jewish Scriptures. This was around 400 B.C. After ten centuries of hearing from God through Moses and other prophets and writers, Israel went through a period of 400 years where God was silent.

After Philip II of Macedonia (born in 382 B.C.) who reigned since 359 B.C. was assassinated in 336 B.C., his son Alexander took over at the age of twenty. Alexander the Great reigned from 336 B.C. to 323 B.C. He conquered Jerusalem from the Persians in 331 B.C. Eventually, he conquered all of the area around Jerusalem as well before he died at the age of 33 years. The Greeks ruled Israel until Pompey conquered Jerusalem for the Romans in 63 B.C. While the Jews were under Grecian rule they were being bombarded by religious and cultural Hellenistic changes. One of the cultural changes was the emergence of Greek as the spoken language.

After Alexander's death the conquered land was divided between his generals; the most powerful were Antigonus, Seleucus, and Ptolemy. The Seleucids from Syria and the Ptolemies from Egypt were not content with their new found inheritance. And, they were fighting to expand their boundaries nearly continually. As a consequence the little region of Israel oscillated between being under gentile Seleucidan and Ptolemaic domination.

Ptolemy II, called Philadelphus, reigned from 285 B.C. to 246 B.C. He wanted to make the Holy Scriptures of the Jews available to all of the Greek speaking world. As a result, he commissioned seventy-two (six from each tribe of Israel) men to conduct a translation of the Holy Scriptures from Hebrew to Greek. They performed the task in seventy-two days. This translation is referred to as the Septuagint or simply as LXX in Roman vernacular.

The Hellenistic reform took on the extreme under the reign of Antiochus IV called Epiphanes (175 B.C. to 163 B.C.). His ordinances were forced on the Jews by punishment of death. Any Jewish boys who were found circumcised were killed and their dead bodies were hung around their mothers neck.

Antiochus IV desecrated the Jewish Temple when he offered a pig as a sacrifice in 167 B.C. This act spurred the Maccabean revolt. John Maccabee and his five sons took up arms against the Antiochean government in guerrilla warfare. The Maccabean revolution won back control of Jerusalem and the temple after the third year of fierce fighting. The temple was re-dedicated to the Lord in 164 B.C. The re-dedication of the temple was memorialized by Israel by establishing another feast day in the Jewish year. This feast is called the Festival of Dedication or the Feast of Lights or Hanukkah.

With the Maccabean victory the Hasmonean era had its beginning. John Hyrcanus was made high-priest of Israel in 135 B.C. Hyrcanus adopted a hard line against Hellenism in defense of Judaism. It was in this setting that a certain Pharisee wrote The Book of Jubilees in Hebrew during the latter part of the second century before the Christian Era (109 B.C.—105 B.C.).(1) [I will also give the world wide web site where the reader can find the pseude-pigraphic or apocryphal writing on the internet. The Book of Jubilees can be found on web site <http://www.ccel.org/c/charles/otpseudepig/jubilee/4.htm>.(10)]

In Jubilees 4:29-30 it reads, And at the close of the nineteenth jubilee, in the seventh week in the sixth year thereof, Adam died, and all his sons buried him in the land of his creation, and he was the first to be buried in the earth. (18 jubilees * 49 years/jubilee + 6 weeks * 7 years/week + 6 years = 930 years.) And he lacked seventy years of one thousand years; for one thousand years are as one day (Ps. 90:4, 2 Pet. 3:8) in the testimony of the heavens and therefore was it written concerning the tree of knowledge: **"On the day that ye eat thereof ye shall die"**. (Gen. 2:17) For this reason he did not complete the years of this day; for he died during it." [Direct quotations of apocryphal writings were underlined rather than put in bold print like the canonized writings. The parenthetical comments have been added by me to help explain the previous text.]

It appears the pre-Messianic Jews believed God gave two definitions for 'day' when He told Adam **". . . for in the day that thou eatest thereof thou shalt surely die."** Adam died spiritually when he ate the fruit of the tree, but he also died physically within a thousand year day. There is no record of anybody living any longer than one thousand years. Methuselah lived the longest at 969 years. Methuselah died the same year that the world-wide flood began.

It is not uncommon that God has two definitions of a thing. God has two definitions of a 'tree'. The living tree with roots, branches and leaves, and a tree made of wood used as a crucifixion cross. The Jews knew that God meant a crucifixion cross. **"And if a man have committed a sin worthy of death, and he be to be put to death, and thou hang him on a tree: his body shall not remain all night upon the tree, but thou shalt in any wise bury him that day; (for he that is hanged is accursed of God;) that thy land be not defiled, which the Lord thy God giveth thee for an inheritance."** (Deut. 21:22-23) The Jews did not want to defile the land which the Lord God gave them when Jesus was crucified. They hurriedly took Jesus down and put Him in a borrowed tomb.

With the prophecy of the coming Messiah yet to be fulfilled, Israel was looking for His reign to be an earthly reign for one thousand years. So when Jesus appeared on the scene the Jews were looking for a King that would set up His throne and put down the Romans as well as all aggressive heathen nations.

II. Christian Era

Jesus had quite a different message than the Pharisees and Sadducees were ready to receive. For many generations the Jewish leaders had been teaching their people **". . . eye for eye, tooth for tooth, hand for hand, foot for foot"**, as stated in Exodus 21:24. Jesus taught that it was better to turn the other cheek which is just what Jesus did when He went to the cross. Jesus answered Pilate when Pilate was trying to worm-out of the predicament that the Jews had placed him in. **"My kingdom is not of this world"** (John 18:36). For indeed, Jesus' kingdom is with a new heavens and a new earth.

Jesus gave impetus to His thousand year reign when He told the Pharisees about King Herod, **"Go ye, and tell that fox, behold, I cast out devils, and I do cures to day and to morrow, and the third day I shall be perfected. Nevertheless I must walk to day, and to morrow, and**

the day following: for it cannot be that a prophet perish out of Jerusalem." (Luke 13:32-33). The prophecy in verse 32 was not about Jesus' death and resurrection. The 'day' spoken of in this prophecy could not have been a 24-hour day because the prophecy was not given on the day before His crucifixion. And in fact, the prophecy was not even given during the week of His crucifixion. It was given sometime around the beginning of His ministry. I maintain 'today and tomorrow' as used here are 'one thousand-year days'. Jesus was foretelling what His job was until the end of this age. For two days or two thousand years He would continue to cast out demons, cure people, and perform miracles. On the third day He will reign on earth with 'perfectness' for one thousand years.

After Jesus' death and resurrection in A.D. 33, the disciples of the Lord were expecting the coming of Christ for His bride, the church, was imminent. The disciples probably assumed that **"This generation shall not pass, till all these things be fulfilled"** in Matthew 24:34 meant them. (No matter that the 40 years that man or beast was not to step foot in Egypt was yet unfulfilled, as stated in Ezekiel 29:8-16. This could be fulfilled during the reign of Christ.) When the temple was destroyed by Titus in A.D. 70 or some time shortly thereafter, the disciples knew that "this generation" did not mean them. The only other interpretation was "this generation" meant the generation that witnessed all the things that took place prior to verse 34 in Matthew 24.

The body of believers (the church) grew rapidly after Christ's resurrection. During the first Pentecost after His ascension, the church grew from one hundred and twenty Jewish men to three thousand Jewish men in one day. Before the first century was over, the word of Jesus' atoning act had spread over all of the Roman empire.

During the early days of the church there was much persecution from the government (Rome) and the Jewish leaders and their followers. Saul, or Paul as he was renamed later, was an avid persecutor of the church until he met Jesus on the road to Damascus. Paul was a Pharisee who studied under Gamaliel, the grandson of the famous Hillel, and was well-versed in Jewish custom and beliefs.

Paul became a highly effective Christian evangelist to the Gentiles. He is responsible for writing 13 or 14 epistles of the New Testament. Paul, throughout his epistles, gave admonition to the believers that the Lord was going to return for His church any day. In other words, Christ's return was imminent. Paul's knowledge of Ezekiel 29 would tell him that Egypt's prophetic message of desolation where **"No foot of man shall pass through it, nor foot of beast shall pass through it, neither shall it be inhabited forty years"**, had not been fulfilled yet. Paul evidently was thinking this prophetic passage of Scripture did not require fulfillment for the imminent return of Christ. He probably assumed that this passage would be fulfilled during Christ's reign on earth or just prior to His reign.

The religious center of Christianity was Jerusalem from A.D. 33 to sometime between 62 and 68. Because the Jews were in conflict with the Romans, Jerusalem was about to be destroyed by the Romans. By God's grace the followers of Christ vacated Jerusalem prior to its destruction. Christians leaders in Jerusalem, by divine revelation and the grace of God, decided to move the church to Pella beyond Jordan.(2) Later Antioch in Syria became the new Christian center.

Jerusalem and the temple were destroyed by the Roman army under Titus in A.D. 70 after a four-month siege.

The Apostle John wrote the book of The Revelation of Jesus Christ around A.D. 96. John lived at Ephesus during his later years. His grave has been reported as being seen in Ephesus. In Revelation 20, John refers to a period of one thousand years in which Satan is bound in chains and thrown into hell. The souls who were faithful to Jesus lived and reigned with Christ—" . . . **and they lived and reigned with Christ a thousand years**" (Rev. 20:4b). This is the millennial reign of Jesus Christ.

The early church was constantly under attack by the Roman authorities who were attempting to appease the Jewish Judaizers. It is believed that all of the eleven original disciples, with the possible exception of John, who were at the Feast of Pentecost forty-nine days after the resurrection were martyred for their faith in Jesus Christ.

This severe persecution of believers by the Roman government lasted for the better part of three centuries until Constantine the Great (A.D. 306—337) established toleration of Christianity through the Edict of Milan in A.D. 313. Some of the early church writers who were martyred for their faith include James the brother of John about A.D. 44 by Herod Agrippa I (Acts 12:1-2); apostle Peter about A.D. 67; apostle Paul about the same time; Ignatius (c.50-c.107) of Antioch in Syria, a disciple of the apostle John; Polycarp (c.69-c.155), appointed by the apostle John to be bishop of Smyrna; Justin Martyr (c.110-c.165), Christian apologist; and Irenaeus (c.130-202), bishop of Lyon. Of these well-known Christian martyrs, Justin Martyr and Irenaeus were admitted millennialist by their own writings which we have today. Other early millennialists include Papias (c.70—c.155), Tertullian (Quintus Septimius Florens Tertullianus) (c.155-c.245), who was ordained a priest at Carthage in North Africa (not martyred), Hippolytus, Methodius, Commodianus, and Lactantius.(3)

Early Christians who were opposed to a belief in a millennial reign of Christ were Origen (c.185-c.254), Dionysius of Alexandria (c.200-c.265), Eusebius (c.260-c.341), and Augustine (354-430). Dionysius was a student of Origen.

Origen, a student of Clement of Alexandria Egypt, was a priest at Caesarea in Palestine at age 18. He was the author of the Hexapla, a six columned Old Testament. Origen was trying to protect Christians against the charge that they had falsified the Biblical texts. The Hexapla was about 6500 pages long. It was never copied. The Hexapla was destroyed in the seventh century.

Eusebius Pamphilus wrote on the history of the early church. He acknowledges the proponents of millennialism as well as those who were opposed to it.

St. Augustine identified the Church with the Kingdom of God and maintained that the millennial age had already come. Many of St. Augustine's views were adopted by the Catholic church and ultimately by Protestant reformers. Martin Luther who was active during the early part of the sixteenth century was a great reformer. He was an Augustinian friar.

Papias was the bishop of Hierapolis (now called Pammukale in Phrygia, Turkey) and a companion of Polycarp during the first half of the second century. (4) He provided important apostolic oral source accounts of the history of early Christianity and of the origins of the Gospel. According to Irenaeus, the leading theologian of the second century, Papias was believed to have known and conversed with the apostle John and the apostle Philip. Eusebius of Caesarea in Palestine, in his book "Historia Ecclesiastica" (Church History), supports Irenaeus' claim. John was believed to have spent his waning years in Ephesus where Irenaeus claimed his grave existed. Ephesus is less than a hundred miles from the historical Hierapolis. Tradition has also placed Philip's death and burial at Hierapolis. Papias wrote articles (ca. 130) which are now almost extant called "Explanation of the Sayings of the Lord". Papias was noted for his apocalyptic teaching of Christ returning to change the world into a thousand-year era of universal peace. Fragments of Papias from Eusebius, Hist. Eccl., Book 3, Chapter 39 reveal "... there will be a millennium after the resurrection from the dead, when the personal reign of Christ will be established on this earth." His teaching goes along with John's writings in the book of Revelation 20:4b. [See web site, <http://www.ccel.org/ccel/schaff/anf01.html> for the Fragment VI of Papias.]

The Epistle of Barnabas is also an early non-canonical Christian writing. It is estimated to have been written after the destruction of the temple in A.D. 70 and before Hadrian rebuilt Jerusalem following the revolt in A.D. 132-135. The epistle is generally thought to have originated in Alexandria, Egypt. (5) Whether this is the Barnabas who traveled with the apostle Paul can not be confirmed. Eusebius says he was one of the seventy disciples (Luke 10) sent out by the Lord. (6)

The Epistle of Barnabas reads, "Of the sabbath He speaketh in the beginning of the creation; and God made the works of His hands in six days, and He ended on the seventh day, and rested on it, and He hallowed it. Give heed, children, what this meaneth; He ended in six days. He meaneth this, that in six thousand years the Lord shall bring all things to an end; for the day with Him signifieth a thousand years; and this He himself beareth me witness, saying; behold, the day of the Lord shall be as a thousand years. Therefore, children, in six days, that is in six thousand years, everything shall come to an end. And He rested on the seventh day." (Barn. 15:3-5)

"It is not your present sabbaths that are acceptable [unto Me], but the sabbath which I have made, in the which, when I have set all things at rest, I will make the beginning of the eighth day which is the beginning of another world. Wherefore also we keep the eighth day for rejoicing, in the which also Jesus rose from the dead, and having been manifested ascended into the heavens." (The Epistle of Barnabus 15:8-9, written between A.D. c.70-c.130, APOSTOLIC FATHERS (trans. and ed., J. B. Lightfoot))

The Epistle of Barnabas tells of 6000 years as the 6-days of the world + 1000 years as the 7th day or Sabbath of the Lord. The eighth day is the period between 7000 and 8000 years and will be the first day of a new week of another world. This can be taken as the beginning of a blissful state which we call heaven where time is eternal.

The argument that Barnabus puts forth **"In that day on which ye shall eat of it, ye shall die by death"** is that Christ was crucified on the sixth day (Friday), the same day that Adam ate of the forbidden fruit and died. This assumes that Adam and Eve ate of the tree of knowledge of good and evil the same day of the week that they were created, i.e., the sixth day of a subsequent week. [Epistle of Barnabus, Chapter XV can also be found on web site <http://www.ccel.org/ccel/schaff/anf01.html>.]

Justin Martyr writes in Chapters 80 and 81 of his "Dialogue with Trypho" for the Christians addressed to the Roman Senate in response to those who do not believe in the millennial reign of Christ. But I and others, who are right-minded Christians on all points, are assured that there will be a resurrection of the dead, and a thousand years in Jerusalem, which will then be built, adorned, and enlarged,[as] the prophets Ezekiel and Isaiah and others declare.

For Isaiah spake thus concerning this space of a thousand years: **"For there shall be the new heaven and the new earth, and the former shall not be remembered, or come into their heart; but they shall find joy and gladness in it, which things I create. For, Behold, I make Jerusalem a rejoicing, and My people a joy; and I shall rejoice over Jerusalem, and be glad over My I people. And the voice of weeping shall be no more heard in her, or the voice of crying. And there shall be no more there a person of immature years, or an old man who shall not fulfil his days. For the young man shall be an hundred years old; but the sinner who dies an hundred years old, he shall be accursed. And they shall build houses, and shall themselves inhabit them; and they shall plant vines, and shall themselves eat the produce of them, and drink the wine. They shall not build, and others inhabit; they shall not plant, and others eat. For according to the days of the tree of life shall be the days of my people; the works of their toil shall abound. Mine elect shall not toil fruitlessly, or beget children to be cursed; for they shall be a seed righteous and blessed by the Lord, and their offspring with them. And it shall come to pass, that before they call I will hear; while they are still speaking, I shall say, What is it? Then shall the wolves and the lambs feed together, and the lion shall eat straw like the ox; but the serpent [shall eat] earth as bread. They shall not hurt or maltreat each other on the holy mountain, saith the Lord."** Now we have understood that the expression used among these words, **"According to the days of the tree [of life] shall be the days of my people; the works of their toil shall abound"** obscurely predicts a thousand years. [Justin quoted Isaiah 65:17-25 out of the Septuagint.]

For as Adam was told that in the day he ate of the tree he would die, we know that he did not complete a thousand years. We have perceived, moreover, that the expression, **"The day of the Lord is as a thousand years,"** is connected with this subject. And further, there was a certain man with us, whose name was John, one of the apostles of Christ, who prophesied, by a revelation that was made to him, that those who believed in our Christ would dwell a thousand years in Jerusalem; and that thereafter the general, and, in short, the eternal resurrection and judgment of all men would likewise take place. Just as our Lord also said, **"They shall neither marry nor be given in marriage, but shall be equal to the angels, the children of the God of the resurrection."** [See web site <http://www.ccel.org/ccel/schaff/anf01.html> for Justin Martyr's "Dialogue with Trypho", Chapters 80 and 81.]

Another Christian non-canonical writing called "The Vision of Paul" or "Apocalypse of Paul" also gives credence to the millennial theory. This writing was supposedly written by the Apostle Paul relating his experience when he was caught up to the third heaven as referred to in II Cor. 12:2. **"I know a man in Christ who fourteen years ago—whether in the body I do not know, or whether out of the body I do not know, God knows—such a one was caught up to the third heaven."** The writing was discovered by a resident in the foundation of the home where Paul lived in Tarsus some 320 years earlier. The writing was passed on to the Roman emperor Theodosius the Great who ruled from A.D. 379 to 395. "The Vision of Paul", Chapter 21 reads, "The angel answered and said to me, When Christ, whom thou preachest, shall come to reign, then, by the sentence of God, the first earth will be dissolved and this land of promise will then be revealed, and it will be like dew or cloud, and then the Lord Jesus Christ, the King Eternal, will be manifested and will come with all his saints to dwell in it, and he will reign over them a thousand years, and they will eat of the good things which I shall now show unto thee." ["The Vision of Paul", Chapter 21 can be found with the Google search engine at web site <http://www.ccel.org/ccel/schaff/anf09.html>.]

Irenaeus in Book V, "Irenaeus Against Heresies", writes in Chapter 23. And there are some, again, who relegate the death of Adam to the thousandth year; for since "a day of the Lord is as a thousand years," he did not overstep the thousand years, but died within them, thus bearing out the sentence of his sin. Whether, therefore, with respect to disobedience, which is death; whether [we consider] that, on account of that, they were delivered over to death, and made debtors to it; whether with respect to [the fact that on] one and the same day on which they ate they also died (for it is one day of the creation); whether [we regard this point], that, with respect to this cycle of days, they died on the day in which they did also eat, that is, the day of the preparation, which is termed "the pure supper," that is, the sixth day of the feast, which the Lord also exhibited when He suffered on that day; or whether [we reflect] that he (Adam) did not overstep the thousand years, but died within their limit,—it follows that, in regard to all these significations, God is indeed true. For they died who tasted of the tree; and the serpent is proved a liar and a murderer, as the Lord said of him: "For he is a murderer from the beginning, and the truth is not in him." [See web site < http://www.ccel.org/ccel/schaff/anf01.html> for Book v of "Irenaeus Against Heresies", Chapter 23.]

If a day equals one thousand years like the Jews, early church fathers, and millennialists thought, and not a thousand years equal to one day as the later church fathers and amillennialists believed, it becomes desirable to know the age of the earth. The age of the earth can not be determined with certainty, but only approximated even with the Holy Scriptures.

In order to approximate the age of the earth, we need to know when the world was created relative to some reference year that we are familiar with. The modern day populace have adopted Ussher's reference year as 4004 B.C. and I will do likewise. James Ussher (1581-1656) was an Irish Archbishop who helped lead Ireland through the Protestant Reformation. Ussher used the Masoretic text when deriving the year of 4004 B.C. for creation.

The Jews have established that God created the world 3761 years before the Christian Era, or 3761 B.C. In fact, they say God created the world Tishri 1, 3761(Sept/Oct 3761). I was unable to find out how they calculated that date—never mind with such accuracy. If the chronology was performed any other time than between the third century before the Christian Era to the second century of the Christian Era, which I suspect it was, the Hebrew Text which later became known as the Masoretic Text would have undoubtedly been used.

The dead sea scrolls (7) gave proof that there were at least three texts of the Bible prior to 250 B.C. One was the standard Hebrew text which later became known as the Masoretic Text (MT); one was the Hebrew text which was translated into the Greek Septuagint (LXX). The third one was the first five books of the Tanach and known as the Samaritan Pentateuch (SP).

The Septuagint differs extensively with the Hebrew text, or what later was referred to as the Masoretic text. The ages of the patriarchs when they begat their successor is often inflated by 100 years in the Septuagint. The Septuagint also has an additional patriarch between Arphaxad and Salah by the name of Cainan. These differences are shown in Figure 1. The Alexandrine version of the Septuagint text has a total of 3394 years compared to 2008 years, or 1386 additional years over the progeneration given in the Hebrew (or Masoretic) text in Genesis 5 and 11. [<http://www.netrover.com/~numbers/chron_3.html>]

Progenitors—Masoretic Text/Septuagint Text*	Age of Earth in Years Masoretic Text /Septuagint Text	
God created Adam	**0**	**0**
Adam begat Seth when he was 130/230	130	230
Seth begat Enosh when he was 105/205	235	435
Enosh begat Cainan when he was 90/190	325	625
Cainan begat Mahalaleel when he was 70/170	395	795
Mahalaleel begat Jared when he was 65/165	460	960
Jared begat Enoch when he was 162/162	622	1122
Enoch begat Methuselah when he was 65/165	687	1287
Methuselah begat Lamech when he was 187/187	874	1474
Lamech begat Noah when he was 182/188	1056	1662
Noah begat Shem when he was 502/502	1558	2164
<<<<<<<<<Flood>>>>>>>>>	**1656**	**2262**
Shem begat Arphaxad when he was 100/100	1658	2264
<<<<<Arphaxad begat Cainan when he was—/135	------	2399
<<<<<Cainan begat Salah when he was—/130	------	2529
Arphaxad begat Salah when he was 35/—	1693	------
Salah begat Eber when he was 30/130	1723	2659
Eber begat Peleg when he was 34/134	1757	2793
Peleg begat Reu when he was 30/130	1787	2923
Reu begat Serug when he was 32/132	1819	3055
Serug begat Nahor when he was 30/130	1849	3185
Nahor begat Terah when he was 29/79	1878	3264
Terah begat Abram when he was 130/130****	**2008**	**3394**

* Alexandrine version of the Septuagint text.

** Calculated from Gen. 11:31-32, 12:4 & Acts 7:4 to be 130 years instead of 70 years.

Figure 1

By adding 1386 to Ussher's date for creation of 4004 B.C., you get 5390 B.C.

The Vaticanus version of the Septuagint text gives a smaller difference of only 29 years. This version has an error in maintaining a correct chronological sequence of events. For example, Methuselah dies fourteen years after the flood.

The first Christian historian known to produce a universal chronology was Sextus Julius Africanus. (8) Africanus was born around A.D. 180 in Jerusalem. His life is not well documented, but evidence indicates that Africanus traveled considerably in Asia, Egypt, and Italy and later lived chiefly at Emmaus, in Palestine, where he served as prefect. He was named regional ambassador to Rome, when he became a protege of the Roman emperor Severus Alexander. Africanus' greatest work was "Chronographiai" written about A.D. 221. It was a five-volume treatise on sacred and profane history from the Creation which he found to be 5499 years before the birth of Christ. Relying on the Bible and other books of that day as the basis of his calculations, he incorporated and synchronized Egyptian and Chaldaean chronologies, Greek mythology, and Judaic history with Christianity. His work raised the prestige of early Christianity by placing it within a historical context. [See web site <http://www.newadvent. org/fathers/0614.htm > for Africanus' chronology.]

It is apparent that Africanus used the Septuagint to base his calculations. The date of 5390 B.C. is only 109 years less than 5499 B.C., which is the year Africanus said that God created all things. After all, the Greek version was the most commonly used translation of the Old Testament for the early church during the first six centuries of the Christian era. His chronology for calculating the age of the earth falls very close to the approximate age that most Christians (at that time) assumed for the creation.

Although Africanus relied heavily on the Septuagint and other profane historical books he did perform a service of influencing the thinking of that day. Many early Christian men, like Eusebius, thought of the world's existence as being 5000 to 5500 years before the birth of Christ. Just as Ussher has influenced the people in the last three centuries. The transition was due mainly by the changing of the canon from the Septuagint Text to the Masoretic Text. When Christian people stopped adopting the canon of the Old Testament as the Septuagint and started recognizing the Masoretic Text as canon they went from accepting the creation as being around 5000 to 5500 B.C. to around 3700 to 4200 B.C. Did the recognition of the Masoretic Text over the Septuagint Text as sacred come first, or did the fact that the Lord did not make His return appearance, as supposed, at A.D. 500 to 1000 come first?

To summarize the above discussion, the following table was made up showing the different thoughts based on the canon in that day as to the age of the earth at the birth of Christ. [<http:// www.netrover.com/~numbers/chron_3.html>.]

Source	Estimated Year of Creation
Jewish faith	3761 B.C., Jewish Era (probably based on Hebrew Text)
Present church	4004 B.C., Ussher (based on Masoretic Text)
Early church	5198 B.C., Eusebius (based on Septuagint Text)
Early church	5499 B.C., Africanus (based on Septuagint Text)
Early church	5508 B.C., Byzantine Era (based on Septuagint Text)

Summary

1. The doctrine of the reign of the Messiah on earth is older than the Christian Era.

Isaiah expresses the teaching plainly in his writing (Isa. 66:22-24). Ezekiel and Zechariah substantiate what Isaiah had to say.

2. The teaching of a day being equivalent to one thousand years in God's schedule is not a new doctrine. Psalm 90:4 was written approximately 1400 B.C. by Moses.

Neither is the duration of this age as being 6 days equal to 6000 years. Nor is the Lord's day, being the 7th day, equivalent to 6000—7000 years, a new teaching. These teachings had their beginning with the Jews at least a century before the birth of Christ, if not more. These teachings were promulgated down through the ages by the early church. The assurance of such a millennium was carefully taught by a succession of church fathers from Justin Martyr and Papias, who conversed with the immediate disciples of the apostles, and Irenaeus down to Lactantius, who was preceptor to the son of Constantine. (8)

3. The early church from its inception to A.D. 400 or 500 taught from the Septuagint that they were approaching the 6000th year of history.

The early church of Antioch computed almost 6000 years from the creation of the world to the birth of Christ. Africanus, Lactantius, and the Greek church have reduced that number to 5500, and Eusebius has convinced himself with 5200 years. These calculations were formed on the Septuagint, which was universally received by the Christians during the first six centuries. (8)

4. The Jews rejected the Septuagint in favor of the Hebrew text around A.D. 100-200.

The Jewish community rejected the Septuagint as being corrupted around the start of the second century. They preferred the Hebrew Text as their canon.

Originally, the Hebrew Manuscripts had no vowels in its alphabet, no accents, and no punctuations. Vowel sounds, accents, and punctuations were for the most part handed down by tradition. The process of adding the vowel sounds, accents, and punctuations into the reading of the Old Testament is called Masorah. The Masorah comes from the Hebrew root word masar which is a verb that means 'to hand down'. It was not till later on that the name Masoretes, was given to those people who were the preservers of Masorah. During the Talmudic period (c. A.D. 300-500), the rules for perpetuating Masorah were extremely detailed. Around the tenth century, the written Masorah version of the Hebrew Text was completed to form what we call the Masoretic Text.

5.   The early Catholic church gave up the '6 days equal to 6000 years' teaching before they gave up on the Septuagint and adopted the Hebrew or Masoretic Text as canon.

The Masoretic Text of the Old Testament and the Greek Vulgate of the New Testament have since become the authority for scripture of Catholics and Protestants.

6.   I believe we are approaching the 6000th year of history.

To summarize the thoughts in this document I will quote Edward Gibbon from his book 'The Decline and Fall of the Roman Empire' when talking about those believers who followed the Septuagint Text. "The ancient and popular doctrine of the Millennium was intimately connected with the second coming of Christ. As the works of the creation had been finished in six days, their duration in their present state, according to a tradition which was attributed to the prophet Elijah, was fixed to six thousand years. By the same analogy it was inferred that this long period of labour and contention, which was now almost elapsed, would be succeeded by a joyful Sabbath of a thousand years; and that Christ, with the triumphant band of the saints and elect who had escaped death, or who had been miraculously revived, would reign upon earth till the time appointed for the last and general resurrection."[9]

References:

(1)   The Book of Jubilees, The Apocrypha and Pseudepigrapha of the Old Testament in English, Volume II—Pseudepigrapha by R. H. Charles, Oxford University Press First Published 1913, 1979 Edition

(2)   The Ecclesiastical History, of Eusebius, Book 3, Chapter 5

(3)   The Meaning of Millennium by Robert G. Clouse, page 9

(4)   The New Encyclopaedia Britannica, Volume 9, page 128

(5)   The Apostolic Fathers. Second Edition, J. B. Lightfoot, J. R. Harmer, M. W. Holmes, Introduction

(6)   The Ecclesiastical History, of Eusebius Pamphilus, Book 1, Chapter 12

(7)   The Mystery and Meaning of the Dead Sea Scrolls, Hershel Shanks

(8)   The New Encyclopaedia Britannica, Volume 1, page 136

(9)   The Decline and Fall of the Roman Empire by Edward Gibbon, Volume 1, Chapter XV, Section ii

(10) The web sites given in this document were active in the summer of 2003. I have no control as to the status of these web sites, so they may be changed or no longer in service at the time the reader wants to refer to them.

CHAPTER 4
A LUTHERAN'S VIEW ON ESCHATOLOGY

When I was growing up in South Dakota my folks had me baptized as an infant, took me to church, and sent me to Sunday school and confirmation class, which I am forever grateful. When in the seventh and eighth grades (Sept., 1945—May, 1947), I was instructed in good Lutheran theology, which I accepted without reservation. That is, until I was about 30 years old. Then, I began to question the Lutheran view on <u>end time</u> events. In particular, the teaching that a) New Testament Christians are the new Israel, which is just another way of saying, God is through with the Jewish nation, b) the end of the world comes instantaneously to everyone at the Lord's second coming, and c) there isn't a <u>millennial age</u>, or reign of Christ, on earth. I no longer accept these teachings as being Biblical. I believe God is fulfilling prophecy through the Jewish nation, Israel, today. And, the calling out of His saints in the rapture and Christ's millennial reign are a part of these eschatological events. I will address these three theological issues below.

The Biblical references are taken from the New King James version. Direct quotations are in bold print.

a) God is not through with the Jewish nation

A Jewish remnant is discussed in Isaiah, Jeremiah, Ezekiel, Joel, Amos, Micah, Habakkuk, Zephaniah, Haggai, Zechariah. The remnant is a special people who have received or are to receive God's grace and forgiveness. On that day of at-one-ment, at the end of the <u>great tribulation</u>, Christ will heal the Jewish nation. (The tribulation is a period of approximately seven years. The great tribulation is the last three and one-half years of the seven-year period. Christ will return to earth at the end of the great tribulation.)

Zech. 12:10
"And I will pour on the house of David and on the inhabitants of Jerusalem the Spirit of grace and supplication; then they will look on Me whom they have pierced; they will mourn for Him as one mourns for his only son, and grieve for Him as one grieves for a firstborn."

Isaiah 10:22-23
For though your people, O Israel, be as the sand of the sea, yet a remnant of them will return; the destruction decreed shall overflow with righteousness. For the Lord God of hosts will make a determined end in the midst of all the land.

Lest one may think God is talking just about the remnant returning from Assyria or Babylon, Paul quotes Isaiah in **Rom. 9:27** as if it applies for the future.

Isaiah 49:15
"Can a woman forget her nursing child, and not have compassion on the son of her womb? Surely they may forget, yet I will not forget you.

Jeremiah 31:36
"If those ordinances depart from before Me," says the Lord, "Then the seed of Israel shall also cease from being a nation before Me forever."

Romans 11:25-27
For I do not desire, brethren, that you should be ignorant of this mystery, lest you should be wise in your own opinion, that hardening in part has happened to Israel until the fullness of the Gentiles has come in. And so all Israel will be saved, as it is written: "The Deliverer will come out of Zion, and He will turn away ungodliness from Jacob; for this is My covenant with them, when I take away their sins."

Genesis 17:7
The Abrahamic covenant is an everlasting covenant.

b)   Rapture

I Thess. 4:13-18
The saved people (Christians) will rise up to meet the Lord in the air, and thus we shall always be with the Lord. (These passages don't say anything about the unsaved, or non-Christians.) This departing of the saints will be "in a twinkling of an eye" (**I Cor. 15:52**), or rapere. Thus, the word rapture comes from the Latin word rapere.

Isaiah 4:2
In that day the Branch of the Lord shall be beautiful and glorious; and the fruit of the earth shall be excellent and appealing for those of Israel who have escaped.

I believe, the phrase, 'For those of Israel who have escaped', is referring to the people caught up in the rapture and escaped the tribulation.

Acts 1:6-7
The disciples asked Him, **"Lord, will You at this time restore the kingdom of Israel?" And He said to them, "It is not for you to know times or seasons which the Father has put in His own authority."**

The kingdom of Israel is different than the kingdom of heaven. The Lord did not rebuke them.

Isaiah 57:1 (pre-tribulation rapture)
The righteous perishes (disappear) **and no man takes it to heart; merciful men are taken away, while no one considers that the righteous is taken away from evil.**

The same thing happened to Noah and the other seven with him. They were caught up seven days prior to the flood coming. God shut the door of the ark seven days prior to the rain coming.

<u>Micah 7:2</u> (people who missed the rapture go through the tribulation)
The faithful man has perished (disappeared) **from the earth, and there is no one upright among men. They all lie in wait for blood; Every man hunts his brother with a net.**

<u>Isaiah 26:20-21</u>
Come, my people, enter your chambers, and shut your doors behind you; hide yourself, as it were, for a little moment, until the indignation is past. For behold, the Lord comes out of His place to punish the inhabitants of the earth for their iniquity; the earth will also disclose her blood, and will no more cover her slain.

This probably is referring to His people left behind after the rapture because it reads 'shut your doors behind you'. I believe God would have shut the door if they were taken in the rapture.

If you are one who believes the rapture gives people a second chance then think again.

<u>II Thess. 2:1-12</u>
Verse 7 tells us what will happen when '. . . **only He** (Holy Spirit) **who now restrains will do so until He** (Holy Spirit) **is taken out of the way.'** The coming lawless one (the antichrist) will have a field day. **And for this reason God will send them strong delusion, that they should believe the lie, that they all may be condemned who did not believe the truth but had pleasure in unrighteousness (vs. 11 & 12).**

I believe it will be just as hard or harder for the unsaved, especially the so-called Christians, after the rapture to come to accept Christ as it was for the Pharisees, <u>Sadducees</u> and other Jews to accept Christ during these last 2000 years.

c)   <u>Millennial reign of Christ on the earth</u>

Ezekiel 29:8-16
God will make the land of Egypt desolate (uninhabited) for forty years. Neither foot of man or beast shall pass through the land. The people of Egypt will be scattered among the nations. At the end of the forty years He will gather them back into the land of Egypt.

This has never happened. It could happen easily with the weapons of mass destruction available today. Radioactive, chemical, or biological freeze-out is a real possibility.

If the world comes to an end with one big bang then we have at least 40 years left, and probably much more because the Egyptians will need to be gathered back into the land. Therefore, Christ's coming for His Church, the bride, would not be imminent.

Zechariah 14:1-21

God will gather all the nations to battle against Jerusalem (vs. 2) (tribulation). Christ returns with all His saints (vs. 5 and Rev. 19:14) (end of the great tribulation). Christ begins His reign as King over all the earth (vs. 9). Everyone who is left of all the nations which came against Jerusalem shall go up from year to year to worship the King (the Lord) and keep the Feast of Tabernacles (vs. 16). Whichever of the families of the earth do not, there will be no rain (vs. 17). If the family of Egypt will not go up to worship the Lord, they will get no rain and instead will receive a plague (vs. 18) (during Christ's millennial reign).

Isaiah 65:17-25 (during Christ's millennial reign)

The Lord will create a new heavens and a new earth (vs. 17). A child shall die one hundred years old, but the sinner being one hundred years old shall be accursed (vs. 20). They shall not labor in vain, nor bring forth children for trouble; for they shall be the descendants of the blessed of the Lord, and their offspring with them (vs. 23). The wolf and the lamb shall feed together, the lion shall eat straw like the ox, and dust shall be the serpent's food (vs. 25).

Isaiah 66:22-23 (during Christ's millennial reign)

"For as the new heavens and the new earth which I will make shall remain before Me," says the Lord, "So shall your descendants and your name remain. And it shall come to pass that from one New Moon to another, and from one Sabbath to another, all flesh shall come to worship before Me," says the Lord.

There is no sun or moon in Heaven. See **Rev. 21:23**.

Ezekiel 40 through 48 (during Christ's millennial reign)

This is talking about the millennial age which has not happened yet.

A new city, Jerusalem, and a new temple will be built. The city will be the highest point around. A spring of water will flow out of the temple eastward toward the Dead Sea which is no longer dead, but teaming with fish. The priests will offer burnt grain and animal sacrifices on the temple altar on New Moons, Sabbaths, and feast days, such as, Unleavened Bread (Passover) and Tabernacles. Levites will work in the temple. The land will be divided up between the twelve tribes of Israel. The boundaries are given. The prince has special laws governing him and his sons.

Because there is death (44:31), marriage and divorce (44:22), and widows (44:22), this can't be Heaven.

Revelation 20 (Christ's millennial reign)

This is after the tribulation talked about in Rev. 4 through 19 and ending with the return of Christ (referred to as Christ's Second Coming). Christ throws the antichrist and false prophet into the lake of fire. Satan is bound for a thousand years. The thousand years is mentioned six times in Chapter 20. This is Christ's millennial reign. It is also called the millennial age in contrast to the age we are in.

I think some scriptural passages, such as, Isaiah 4, Isaiah 11, and Isaiah 35, could be referring to the millennial age, but they are difficult to prove without associating them with a passage already given.

Many more passages are ciphered. For example, the account on the Mount of Transfiguration is ciphered. Matthew 17:1 "After six days . . . .". Mark 9:2 "After six days . . . .". Luke "About eight days . . . .". This makes sense if you accept Psalm 90:4 and II Peter 3:8 as literal. One day equals a thousand years.

Supporting evidence

Genesis 2:16-17
And the Lord God commanded the man, saying, "Of every tree of the garden you may freely eat; but the tree of the knowledge of good and evil you shall not eat, for in the day that you eat of it you shall surely die."

I agree that 'in the day that', Adam died spiritually. But he did not die physically until he was 930 years old. Does God have two definitions for a day?

He does have two definitions for a day. See **II Pet. 3:8. But, beloved, do not forget this one thing, that with the Lord one day is as a thousand years, and a thousand years as one day.**

Several apocryphal writings have this age lasting 6000 years. The seventh day, or from 6000 to 7000 years, will be a day of rest. The Epistle of Barnabas, Fragments of Papias, and The Book of Jubilees are three such books.

The Epistle of Barnabas is believed to have been written in the first half of the second century.

The Epistle of Barnabas, chapter 15, verses 5-14
Of the sabbath He speaketh in the beginning of the creation; And God made the works of His hands in six days, and He ended on the seventh day, and rested on it, and He hallowed it. Give heed, children, what this meaneth; He ended in six days. He meaneth this, that in six thousand years the Lord shall bring all things to an end; for the day with Him signifieth a thousand years; and this He himself beareth me witness, saying; Behold, the day of the Lord shall be as a thousand years. Therefore, children, in six days, that is in six thousand years, everything shall come to an end. And He rested on the seventh day.

Papias was the bishop of Hierapolis and a companion to Polycarp, bishop of Smyrna who was martyred around AD 156. Papias provides some of the very earliest testimony about the early church's stance on the millennium and the authorship of Matthew, Mark, John, and Revelation. Papias mentions two Johns in the same sentence. One called John and another called the elder John.

Fragments of Papias
" . . . there will be a millennium after the resurrection from the dead, when the personal reign of Christ will be established on this earth."

The <u>Book of Jubilees</u> is believed to have been written by a Pharisee during the second century before the Christian Era.

<u>The Book of Jubilee, chapter 4, verses 30-31</u>

And he (Adam) lacked seventy years of one thousand years; for one thousand years are as one day in the testimony of the heavens and therefore was it written concerning the tree of knowledge: 'On the day that ye eat thereof ye shall die.' For this reason he did not complete the years of this day; for he died during it.

All glory and praise be to God and His Son, the Lord Jesus Christ, who He raised from the dead so that I might have eternal life.

CHAPTER 5

ON THE ROAD TO THE 7TH MILLENNIUM

A fairly recent event in Israel brought to the chalkboard an age old problem. In 1996, Israel celebrated the 3000th anniversary of making Jerusalem the capital of Israel by King David. This declaration assumes some knowledge by the Israelis for arriving at their decision. If the Israelis are correct in establishing the year 1005 B.C. as the year that Jerusalem became Israel's capital, then we can get a handle on the age of the world, and consequently, on the end of the 6th millennium. How the Israelis calculated the year when Jerusalem became the capital of Israel is not known for sure but the date does agree within one year of Edwin R. Thiele's 'The Mysterious Numbers of the Hebrew Kings'.

Using 1996 as the starting date, one can approximate the end of this age. In fact, the later year for the end of the age can be calculated. But first, two major events of Scripture have to be dated, in particular, the birth of Abraham and God's covenant with Abraham. Figure 1 is the method used for calculating the start of the 7th millennium. Figure 3 shows the chronology of Biblical events from creation.

First date	1996 A.D.	The year Jerusalem celebrates its 3000th anniversary
	-3000 years	
Second date	1005 B.C.	The year David moved the capital of Israel from Hebron to Jerusalem (subtracting 1 year for going from A.D. to B.C.)
Second date	1005 B.C.	David reigned for 33 yr. + Solomon for 3 yr. before the Temple was built
	-36 years	
Third date	969 B.C.	The year King Solomon starts building the Temple
Third date	969 B.C.	Temple construction was started 480 years after the Israelites left Egypt
	+480 years	
Fourth date	1449 B.C.	The year of the Exodus
Fourth date	1449 B.C.	Israelites left Egypt 430 years after the Abrahamic covenant
	+430 years	
Fifth date	1879 B.C.	The year of the Abrahamic covenant
Fifth date	1879 B.C.	God made a covenant with Abraham when he was 85 years old
	+85 years	
Sixth date	1964 B.C.	The year Abraham was born

Sixth date	1964 B.C.	Abraham was born 2008 years after the world was created
	+2008 years	
Seventh date	3972 B.C.	God created the world
	6000 years	End of the 6th millennium
	-3972 B.C.	
	2029 A.D.	The start of the 7th millennium
		(adding 1 year for going from B.C. to A.D.)

Figure 1

The chronology of events in Scripture is based on the Masoretic text of the Bible. I am well aware of the life span and lineage's of the patriarchs being different in the Septuagint from those in the Masoretic writings. I believe the Greek translation of the Bible has errors in it. The Jews of the second century of the Christian Era probably did too. They abandoned the Septuagint in favor of the Masoretic text.

Abraham's (Abram's) birth
The number of years between creation and Terah, Abraham's father, is given in the book of Genesis. Terah was born 1878 years after creation.

Gen. 11:26 reads, **"And Terah lived seventy years, and begat Abram, Nahor, and Haran."**

At first glance, Gen. 11:26 implies that Terah begat Abram when he was 70 years old. Because Abram was mentioned first, one assumes Abram was the first born of Terah. However, further study of this verse and the following verses, especially Genesis 11:32, Genesis 12:4 and Acts 7:4, would lead one to conclude this to be an incorrect interpretation.

If Terah was 70 years old when he begat Abram, and Abram was 75 when he moved his wife and his nephew to Canaan, then this would make Terah 145 years old when Abram moved to Canaan. But, Gen. 11:32 says Terah lived 205 years and died in Haran. This could only happen if Terah lived 60 years after Abram had moved to Canaan. But Acts 7:4 says that Abram moved from Haran to Canaan when his father was dead. Thus, Terah begat Abram when he was 130 years old or older.

The question is, 'Can Terah father a child at the age of 130 years'? Abraham did. In fact, Abraham was older than 137 years. Sarah (Sarai), Abraham's wife, died when Abraham was 137 years old. And then, Abraham married Keturah and had six sons by her. He died at the ripe old age of 175.

If Terah was older than 130 years when he begat Abraham, how much older?

Gen. 11:30 tells us Sarah was barren when Abraham, Sarah, and Abraham's nephew, Lot, moved from Ur of the Chaldees to Haran. This would lead one to conclude that Sarah was at least 40 years old or older (Abraham 50 or more) when they moved to Haran. And Terah would be 180 years old or older.

If Terah had Abraham at an older age than 130, then the world would be older by the difference between Terah's age at the time when he begat Abraham and 130. I tend to believe Abraham moved his family within a year or less after his father's death. Acts 7:4 seems to support this by using the phrase 'when his father was dead'.

Now if we can make the connection between Abraham's birth and the building of the Temple, we will have approximated the age of the world.

Abrahamic covenant
God made a covenant with Abraham, a minimum of five separate times (Gen. 12:1-3, Gen. 12:7, Gen. 13:15, Gen. 15:1-21, and Gen. 17:1-22).

The first was in Haran when Abraham was 75. God promised to give him some land, to be a great nation, and to bless those who bless him and curse those who curse him. (Gen. 12:1-3)

The second time was in Canaan shortly after they arrived. The Lord said, **"Unto thy seed will I give this land: and there builded he an altar unto the Lord, who appeared unto him".** (Gen. 12:7)

The third time was in Canaan after Abraham came back from Egypt where he had gone to escape a famine, and after he and Lot had split up. The Lord said unto Abraham, **"For all the land which thou seest, to thee will I give it, and to thy seed forever".** (Gen. 13:15)

The fourth time was the first time that Abraham questions God. It was before Abraham's tenth year in the land of Canaan; and before Hagar, Sarah's handmaid, became pregnant by Abraham. (Ishmael was born of Hagar when Abraham was 86 years old.) The Lord God reassures Abraham of His covenant plus He promised him to live to a good old age and to give his descendants a land with boundaries. God also told Abraham his descendants would be strangers in a land that is not theirs, and will serve them, and they will be afflicted by them for 400 years, but they will return to this place in the fourth generation. (Gen. 15:1—21)

The fifth time God spoke to Abraham was when he was 99 years old. God reaffirms His former covenant. Abraham is told, for the first time, his heir will be born of Sarah and he will be named Isaac. God says that Isaac and his descendants are to receive the everlasting covenant. (Gen. 17:1—22)

430-year period
The 430-year period is only mentioned twice in Scripture. Once in chapter 12 of the book of Exodus, when the Israelites were leaving Egypt, and again in chapter 3 of Paul's letter to the Galations.

Ex. 12:40-41
Verse 40: **"Now the sojourning of the children of Israel, who dwelt in Egypt, was four hundred and thirty years."**

Verse 41: **"And it came to pass at the end of the four hundred and thirty years, even the selfsame day it came to pass, that all the hosts of the Lord went out from the land of Egypt."**

Verse 40 makes it sound as if Israelites were in Egypt 430 years. This passage is clarified in the third chapter of Galations.

Gal. 3:16-17
Verse 16: **"Now to Abraham and his seed were the promises made. He saith not, And to seeds, as of many; but as of one, And to thy seed, which is Christ."**

Verse 17: **"And this I say, that the covenant, that was confirmed before of God in Christ, the law, which was four hundred and thirty years after, cannot disannul, that it should make the promise of none effect."**

The Law given by God through Moses cannot annul the promise given by God in Christ to Abraham 430 years earlier. Therefore, the 430-year period is a period that began with the Abrahamic covenant and ended with the giving of the Law that occurred only two months after the <u>exodus from Egypt</u>. This author believes it started when Abraham was 85 years old.

What then is meant by the 400-year period mentioned in Genesis 15?

<u>400-year period</u>
The Israelites were not in Egypt 400 years either. The 400 years referred to in Genesis 15 must be talking about Jacob (or Israel) and the Israelite nation, i.e., Abraham's descendants. The <u>nation of Israel</u> was born with the birth of Jacob and the 400-year period ended with the conquest and dividing of Canaan amongst the 12 tribes of Israel. (Josh. 14)

Gen. 15:13 reads **"And he said unto Abram, Know of a surety that thy seed** [Christ] **shall be a stranger in a land that is not theirs** [the nation Israel]**, and shall serve them; and they shall afflict them** [the nation Israel] **four hundred years."** The words in brackets have been added for clarification.

Gen. 15:16 says **"But in the fourth generation they** [the nation Israel] **shall come hither again: for the iniquity of the Amorites is not yet full."**

The genealogies of the <u>tribe of Levi</u> and Judah are given in Scripture, and therefore, the prophecy above can be verified (Gen. 46, Ex. 6, Num. 1, and Matt. 1). The four generations are as follows:

<u>Levi's offspring</u>
<u>Kohath</u>, Gershon and Merari went to Egypt as youths, or at least unmarried.
1. Amram was born in Egypt, died at age 137 years.
2. Aaron was born in Egypt, died at age 123 years.
3. Eleazar born in Egypt, was at least 30 years old.
4. Phinehas was born in Egypt.

<u>Judah's offspring</u>
Perez, Zerah and Shelah went to Egypt.
Hezron went to Egypt when approx. 20 years old.
1. Ram was born in Egypt.
2. <u>Amminadab</u> was born in Egypt.
3. <u>Nahshon</u> born in Egypt, was greater than 20 years old during the Exodus.
4. Salmon was probably born in Egypt, married Rahab, the harlot from Jericho.

The <u>book of Joshua</u> gives Caleb's age when he was sent to spy out Canaan and when the Israelites divided up the land. Caleb was 40 years old when he was sent as a spy (Josh. 14:7). Because he and Joshua were ready to take the land, they were spared from dying in the desert during the forty years when all men over the age 20 died off. Caleb was 85 years old when they divided up the land amongst the twelve tribes (Josh. 14:10).

From the above analysis, the <u>exodus from Egypt</u> occurred 2523 years after the creation. Now to make the link for connecting the exodus with 1005 B.C.

<u>Exodus-to-Temple Period</u>
In II Samuel 5:3, it states that David reigned over Judah 7 years and 6 months in Hebron and then he moved to Jerusalem where he reigned for 33 years over all Israel and Judah. King David's son, Solomon, took over after David's death. King Solomon was responsible for building the Temple. I Kings 6:1 reads, **"And it came to pass in the four hundred eightieth year after the children of Israel had come out of the land of Egypt, in the fourth year of Solomon's reign over Israel, in the month of Zif, which is the second month, that he began to build the house of the Lord"**. So, the Temple was started 33 + 3 = 36 years after David moved to Jerusalem, or 969 B.C. As a result, the exodus from Egypt occurred in 1449 B.C. or 2523 years after creation.

Figure 3 shows the chronology of Biblical events discussed above, along with many other events. The figure gives time in years from creation, in reference to our present calendar, and in reference to Abraham's birth.

This completes the analysis for determining the upper bound on the age of the world. Assuming the Jews were correct in calculating the 3000th anniversary of Jerusalem. Now, I would like to give some other Bible passages that seem to support 2029 A.D. as the start of the <u>seventh millennium</u>.

<u>Supportive Evidence—Prophecy in Luke</u>
Jesus prophesied his second coming to the Pharisees in Luke 13:32 when he told them to **"Go, tell that fox [Herod], 'Behold, I cast out devils and I do cures to day and to morrow, and the third day I shall be perfected.'"**

It should be noted that Jesus is not talking about His resurrection here. This prophecy was given sometime after His ministry had started here on earth. Yet, it was before the week of His crucifixion, so it cannot be referring to His resurrection.

PAGE 30 | ONE NEW MAN

Jesus has been performing miracles for the last two days, or two thousand years. Whereas, people like Peter and Paul performed miracles including healing, casting out demons and raising people from the dead, it was through the power of Jesus that they did this.

The third day I shall be 'perfected' (KJV, NKJV), 'finish' (AAT), or 'reach my goal' (NIV). The footnote in the Pilgrim Study Bible says 'I shall have finished the work that I came to do'. Strong's Concordance gives the definition of the Greek word 'teleioo', as complete, accomplish, consummate, consecrate, finish, fulfill, make perfect.

Figure 2 describes what Luke 13:32 means to me. It fits quite well with the my article on Dating Christ's Death and Resurrection, dated November 27, 1996.

Years from Creation—A.M.	Date	Event
0	3972 B.C.	Creation
4000 - 4001	A.D. 29	First Coming (Jesus began his ministry)
4001 - 5000	29 - 1028	Day 1 (today)
5001 - 6000	1029 - 2028	Day 2 (tomorrow)
6001	2029	Start of the third day (Christ's Second Coming???)

Figure 2

Supportive Evidence—Prophecy in Psalms
Psalm 90 is used quite extensively to prove that a thousand years is like a day (verse 4) but what about verse 10. Verse 10 has something to say too.

Ps. 90:10
"The days of our years are threescore years and ten; and if by reason of strength they be fourscore years, yet is their strength labour and sorrow; for it is soon cut off, and we fly away."

The phrase 'we fly away' could be referring to our flying away in the rapture.

If we add 70 or 80 years to 1948, the year Israel became a nation again, we arrive at the year 2018 or 2028. However, this refers to the rapture, and not to Jesus' Second Coming. If this is the correct interpretation of Scripture the rapture occurs at least 7 years before Jesus Christ's Second Coming but probably after A.D. 2018.

Supportive Evidence—Prophecy in Matthew
Jesus made a very peculiar statement during passion week. He cursed a fig tree because it did not have any fruit on it. An inanimate object——why did he curse a fig tree? This is the only time, that I can recall, in Scripture, that God curses an inanimate object. Besides, fig trees are not likely to have any figs on them when their budding in the spring.

Then, later in the week He tells His disciples the parable of the fig tree. The fig tree, most likely, represents the <u>nation of Israel</u>. Matthew and Luke record this parable.

Matt. 24:32-36

"Now learn a parable of the fig tree; When his [Israel's] branch is yet tender, and putteth forth leaves, ye know that summer is nigh: So likewise ye, when ye shall see all these things, know that it is near, even at the doors. Verily I say unto you, This generation shall not pass, till all these things be fulfilled. Heaven and earth shall pass away, but my words shall not pass away. But of that day and hour knoweth no man, no, not the angels of heaven, but my Father only."

Verses 29-31 of the same chapter tell us what 'all these things' are. Everything that He mentioned in Verse 4 through Verse 31 including the tribulation and Christ's Second Coming.

A reasonably literate person in the Bible during the tribulation should know the week or month or year of Jesus' Second Coming, but not that day and hour.

'This generation' cannot mean the people living in Jesus' day. So, it must mean those people who see the fig tree budding or the birth of Israel as a nation. How long is a generation? It could be 70 or 80 years.

Come Lord Jesus.

Years from Creation	Date (B.C.)	Years from Abraham's birth	Event (from Gen. 5, Gen. 11 or other stated reference)
0	3972	------	Adam created
			SEVENTH DATE
130			Seth born of Adam when he was 130
235			Enos born of Seth when he was 105
325			Cainan born of Enosh when he was 90
395			Mahalaleel born of Cainan when he was 70
460			Jared born of Mahalaleel when he was 65
622			Enoch born of Jared when he was 162
687			Methuselah born of Enoch when he was 65
874			Lamech born of Methuselah when he was 187
930			Adam dies
987			Enoch was taken by God when he was 365 years old
1042			Seth dies at age 912
1056			Noah born of Lamech when he was 182
1140			Enos dies at age 905
1235			Cainan dies at age 910
1290			Mahalaleel dies at age 895
1422			Jared dies at age 962
1558			Shem born of Noah when he was 502
1651			Lamech dies at age 777

1656			Methuselah dies at age 969. Flood begins.
1657			Flood ends
1658			Arphaxad born of Shem 2 years after the flood when he was 100
1693			Salah born of Arphaxad when he was 35
1723			Eber born of Salah when he was 30
1757			Peleg born of Eber when he was 34
1787			Reu born of Peleg when he was 30
1819			Serug born of Reu when he was 32
1849			Nahor born of Serug when he was 30
1878			Terah born of Nahor when he was 29
1996			Peleg dies at age 239
1997			Nahor dies at age 148
2006			Noah dies at age 950
2008	1964	0	Abraham (Abram) born of Terah when he was 130
			SIXTH DATE
		10	(Determined by analysis from Gen. 11:32, Gen. 12:4, Acts 7:4)
2018			Sarah (Sarai) born.
2026			Reu dies at age 239
2049			Serug dies at age 230
2083		75	Terah dies at age 205
2083	1879	85	Abraham, Sarah & Lot leave Haran and dwell in Canaan (Gen. 12:4).
2093			God made covenant with Abraham.
			FIFTH DATE
		86	Start of 430 year period ending with Exodus (Gen. 15:18, Ex. 12:41).
2094			Ishmael born of Abraham & Hagar (Gen. 16:16).
2096		99	Arphaxad dies at age 438
2107		100	Ishmael circumcised (Gen. 17:25). Sodom and Gomorrah destroyed.
2108			Isaac born of Abraham & Sarah when Abraham was 100 (Gen. 21:3-5).
2126		125	Salah dies at age 433
2133		137	Abraham offers Isaac as a sacrifice (Josephus' Antiq.b.1, c.xiii).
2145		140	Sarah dies at age 127 (Gen. 23:1).
2148			Isaac marries Rebekah at age 40 (Gen.25:20).
2158	1804	160	Shem dies at age 600
2168			Jacob (Israel) & Esau born of Isaac when he was 60 (Gen.25:26).
		175	Start of 400 year period prophesied in Gen. 15:13.
			Ends with dividing of The Promised Land.
2183			Abraham dies at age 175 (Gen. 25:7).
2187		200	Eber dies at age 464
2208		223	Esau marries at age 40 (Gen. 26:34).
2231		231	Ishmael dies at age 137 (Gen. 25:17).
2239		238	Jacob flees to Haran and lives there for 20 years.
2246			Jacob weds Leah at age 78; 7 days later weds Rachel(Gen. 29:20-30).

2259		251	Joseph born of Rachel.
			Jacob flees Laban & returns to Canaan after 20 years (Gen. 31:41).
2276		268	Joseph sold into slavery at age 17 (Gen. 37:2).
2288		280	Isaac dies at age 180 (Gen. 35:28).
2289		281	Joseph becomes Egypt's Minister of Agriculture at 30 (Gen. 41:46).
2298		290	Jacob, at age 130, and his posterity move to Egypt after 7 good years and 2 lean years (Gen. 45:11, Gen. 47:9, Gen. 47:28).
2315		307	Jacob dies at age 147 (Gen. 47:28).
2369		361	Joseph dies at age 110 (Gen. 50:26).
2443		435	Moses born.
2523	1449	515	Israel leaves Egypt (the Exodus).
			FOURTH DATE
			End of 430 year period stated in Ex. 12:41.
2562	1410	554	Aaron dies at age 123 (Num. 33:38).
2563	1409	555	Moses dies at age 120 (Deut. 34:7); 30 days later Israel enters Canaan, The <u>Promised Land</u>, after wandering in the wilderness for 40 years.
2568	1404	560	Israel divides Promised Land amongst the 12 tribes (Jos. 14:10).
			End of 400 year period prophesied in Gen. 15:13.
2960	1012	952	David begins his 40-year reign as king of Israel (I Kings 2:11).
2967	1005	959	David makes Jerusalem the capital of Israel (I Kings 2:11).
			SECOND DATE
			3000th Anniv. of David making Jerusalem the capital of Israel in 1996. (No known reference, Possibly Edwin R. Thiele's, "The Mysterious Numbers of Hebrew Kings")
3000	972	992	Solomon begins his 40-year reign as king of Israel (I Kings 11:42).
3003	969	995	Solomon starts temple in the 4th year of his reign (I Kings 6:1)
			THIRD DATE
			480 years after the Exodus (I Kings 6:1).
3010	962	1002	Solomon's temple completed (I Kings 6:38).
	721		Assyria takes the Northern Kingdom of Israel (II Kings 18:10).
	586		Solomon's temple destroyed (II Kings 25).
	516		Zerrubbabel's temple completed (Ezra 6:15).
	444		Command to rebuild Jerusalem (Neh. 2:1, Dan. 9:25).
	396		End of Old Testament prophecy (??)
4001	A.D.29		Jesus began His ministry
4005	A.D.33		Crucifixion of Jesus, the Messiah
4042	A.D.70		Temple destroyed by the Romans
5920	A.D.1948		Israel becomes a nation by a vote of the United Nations
5968	A.D.1996		3000th Anniversary of Jerusalem being the capital of Israel
			START—FIRST DATE
6000	A.D.2028		End of the 6th Millennium (??)
6001	A.D.2029	------	Start of the 7th Millennium (??)

Figure 3: Chronology of Biblical Events

CHAPTER 6
CRITIQUE ON AFRICANUS' CHRONOLOGY

Sextus Julius Africanus was the first Christian historian known to produce a universal chronology.(1) Africanus was born around A.D. 180 in Jerusalem. His life is not well documented, but evidence indicates that Africanus traveled considerably in Asia, Egypt, and Italy and later lived chiefly at Emmaus, in Palestine, where he served as prefect. He was named regional ambassador to Rome, when he became a protégé of the Roman emperor Severus Alexander. Africanus' greatest work was 'Chronographiai' written about A.D. 221.(2) It was a five-volume treatise on sacred and profane history from the Creation which he found to be 5502 years before the Christian Era. Relying on the Septuagint, or a recension of it, as the basis of his calculations, he incorporated and synchronized Egyptian and Chaldean chronologies, Greek mythology, and Judaic history with Christianity. His work raised the prestige of early Christianity by placing it within a historical context.

Chronology of the World According to Africanus
Without knowing for sure what references was used by Africanus it was difficult to determine how he came up with 5531 years between creation and Jesus beginning His ministry on earth. I can only make an educated guess. The references that I think that Africanus had available to him were the Hebrew text, the Samaritan Pentateuch, several versions of the Septuagint, the writings of Josephus, the Apocrypha, and Pseudepigrapha. These references are available to me also except those writings, if any pertaining to the subject, that have since become lost.

The Samaritan Pentateuch and Septuagint texts differ extensively with the Hebrew text, or what later was referred to as the Masoretic text, as to chronology. This difference is shown in Figure 1. The Hebrew text has 1948 years for the interval of time between creation and Abraham's birth. The Samaritan Pentateuch gives 2249 years for the same interval. The Alexandrinus version of the Septuagint has 3334 years. The Vaticanus version has 3414 years. Josephus gives dates but because of their contradictory nature was hard to compare.

The genealogical account given in Genesis 5 and 11 of the Septuagint was undoubtedly the basis for Africanus' pre-Abrahamic chronology. Africanus had the flood occurring in 2262 A.M., which is identical to the year given in the Alexandrian version of the Septuagint. He probably used the Alexandrian version for the genealogical trail of the postdiluvian patriarchs also. Africanus had a time interval from creation to Abraham's birth of 3202 years. This is 132 years less than the Septuagint Alexandrinus. I think Africanus differed with the Septuagint in two areas. First, he had Shem being the progenitor of Arphaxad "after the flood' instead of 'two years after the flood'. This was, I believe, an oversight. And second, I think he left out Cainan as a patriarch. This resulted in another 130 years. This omission was probably on purpose. So, Africanus had the year of Abraham birth as 3202 A.M., whereas the Septuagint Alexandrinus has the year of 3334 A.M. Was this a miscalculation by Africanus? Or was he using another version of the Septuagint Text? A version which possibly agreed with the Hebrew Text in that area or with another writer, such as, Josephus. Josephus (A.D. c.37-c.100) also relied heavily on the Septuagint. Josephus also omitted Cainan as a post-diluvian patriarch.(3) See Figure 1.

Africanus goes on with his chronology. Abraham begot Isaac when he was 100. Isaac begot Jacob when he was 60. Jacob begat Joseph when be was 91 years old. Compare Gen. 41:46-47, 45:6, and 47:9 to verify. Joseph lived 110 years and died. This totals 3563 years from creation to Joseph's death.

	HEB		SP		LXX-A		LXX-B		Josephus	
PATRIARCH	YB	AP	YB	AP	YB	AP	YB	AP	YB	AP
Adam	0	130	0	130	0	230	0	230	0	230
Seth	130	105	130	105	230	205	230	205	230	205
Enosh	235	90	235	90	435	190	435	190	435	190
Cainan	325	70	325	70	625	170	625	170	625	170
Mahalalel	395	65	395	65	795	165	795	165	795	165
Jared	460	162	460	62	960	162	960	162	960	162
Enoch^	622	65	522	65	1122	165	1122	165	1122	165
Methuselah*	687	187	587	67	1287	187	1287	167	1287	187
Lamech	874	182	654	53	1474	188	1454	188	1474	182
Noah	1056	502	707	502	1662	502	1642	502	1656	
Shem	1558	100	1209	100	2164	100	2144	100		
<<Flood>>	1656		1307		2262		2242		2256	
Arphaxad	1658	35	1309	135	2264	135	2244	135	2268	135
Cainan					2399	130	2379	130		
Salah	1693	30	1444	130	2529	130	2509	130	2403	130
Eber	1723	34	1574	134	2659	134	2639	134	2533	134
Peleg	1757	30	1708	130	2793	130	2773	130	2667	130
Reu	1787	32	1838	132	2923	132	2903	132	2797	130
Serug	1819	30	1970	130	3055	130	3035	130	2927	132
Nahor	1849	29	2100	79	3185	79	3165	179	3059	
Terah**	1878	70	2179	70	3264	70	3344	70		70
Abraham***	1948	100	2249	100	3334	100	3414	100	2548	100
Isaac	2048	60	2349	60	3434	60	3514	60		
Jacob	2108		2409		3494		3574			

HEB = Hebrew Text commonly referred to as the Masoretic Text (written sometime before the Christian Era).

SP = Samaritan Pentateuch Text (written between 500 and 200 BCE).

LXX-A = Septuagint Alexandrinus Text (LXX written during the 3rd century BCE; LXX-Codex A is dated to the 5th century CE).

LXX-B = Septuagint Vaticanus Text (LXX written during the 3rd century BCE; LXX-Codex B is dated to the 4th century CE).

Josephus' Antiquities of the Jews (written between 70 and 100 CE)

YB = Year of Birth—A.M.

AP = Age at Propagation.

^ Enoch did not die. God took him.

* LXX-B has Methuselah's death 14 years after the flood.

** Terah was 70 years old when he begat Abram, Nahor, and Haran, but not all three or in that order.

*** Josephus wrote in b.1, c.6, s.5 that Abraham was born in the 292nd year after Deluge. This agrees with the Hebrew Text.

Figure 1: Genealogy of Patriarchs in Genesis

Africanus then shifted the reference from creation (Anno Mundi) to the Olympiad era. He attempted to relate Hebrew history with Greek history. Africanus obtained the date of the Exodus via Greek mythical literature. He measured the time period from Ogygus, a fictional character. Ogygus was said to have survived the devastating flood of Attica, a region around present day Athens. [I could not locate this literature on Ogygus.] Africanus believed that the flood of Attica occurred at the same time as the Exodus.

The chronograph of Attica was related to the first year of the 55th Greek Olympiad. According to Africanus, Cyrus the Great became king of the Persians that year, and in the same year, the Persians ended the 70-year Babylonian captivity of Israel. The first year of the 55th Olympiad is equal to 559 B.C. in the Christian era. [Cyrus reigned from 559 B.C. to 530 B.C. He conquered Babylon in 539 B.C. and wrote his decree in 538 B.C., or shortly thereafter, allowing the Jews to return to Israel.](4)

The first Olympic Games were played on July 17, 776 B.C. The Greek festival became a tradition and was played every four years thereafter until finally abolished after the Olympics in the 4th century of the Christian era. The date of the Olympic festivals was governed by the first full moon after the summer solstice. An Olympiad is the four-year period between two successive Olympic festivals. The year following the Olympic games was the first year of the Olympiad. The year after the first year was the second year of the Olympiad, and so forth. Consequently, the years of an Olympiad would start in July and end in July. The Greeks and many of the nations governed by Greece used Olympiads as a reference for historical events. The formula for converting a year given in reference to the Olympiad era to a year before the birth of Christ is: [780—(4 * Olympiad + year within Olympiad) = B.C.]. If the result is less than or equal to zero then use the formula: [(4 * Olympiad + year within Olympiad + 1)—780 = A.D.]. The reference origin is 780 B.C. These equations account for the fact that there is no 0 year in the Christian era.

The time interval from Ogygus (or from Moses and the Exodus) to Cyrus was broken down into two sub-intervals. Africanus derived 1020 years using Ogygus as the starting point and going to the first Olympiad. The first year of the 55th Olympiad was 217 years after the first Olympiad. Therefore the total time interval was 1237 years.

In another calculation of this interval, Africanus added together seven sub-intervals. He stated: from the exodus to Moses death are 40; Joshua led the Israelites are 25; the time where the elders were judges are 30; the judges whose history is given in the book of Judges are 490; those of the priests Eli and Samuel are 90; those of the successive kings of the Hebrews are 490; and those of captivity are 70 years to the first year of the reign of Cyrus. The total of 40 + 25 + 30 + 490 + 90 + 490 + 70 = 1235 years. The time interval of 1235 years was only 2 years less than the interval calculated earlier so he used 1237 years. [I certainly agree with the 40 and 70 years but Scripture is not clear as to the other intervals of time.]

The next event for making a time measurement was Artaxerxes' command to rebuild Jerusalem. Artaxerxes gave that command in the 20th year of his reign (Neh. 1:1, 2:1 & 2:7-9). Africanus said that Artaxerxes gave that decree in the 4th year of the 83rd Olympiad, or during the 115th year of the Persian empire. This event occurred during the year prior to the summer of (559 B.C.—115 years = 444 B.C.)(4)

Africanus then used the prophecy of 70 'weeks of years' = 490 years given in Daniel (Dan. 9:24-27) to make the last time interval of his chronology. Africanus interpreted the 490 years to mean lunar years. A lunar year is composed of 12 lunar months. Each lunar month is about 29.5 days long. Thus, a lunar year is approximately 354 days. A solar year is about 365 days. The number of solar years in 490 lunar months is: 490 * 354/365 = 475.23 or approx. 475 solar years. Therefore, by adding 475 years to 444 B.C. we get A.D. 32.

Africanus did another calculation for this time interval using the Greek method of measurement. The time interval for his interpretation of Daniel's 70 weeks was measured from the 4th year of the 83rd Olympiad to the 2nd year of the 202nd Olympiad, which was the 16th year of the reign of <u>Tiberius Caesar</u>. From the command to rebuild Jerusalem (780—(4 * 83 + 4) = 444 B.C.) to the 16th year of Tiberius Caesar ((4 * 202 + 2 + 1)—780 = A.D. 31) was 475 years. [I calculate 474 years.]

Africanus relates the 2nd year of the 202nd Olympiad with the 16th year of Tiberius Caesar. Luke 3:1 reads "Now in the fifteenth year of the reign of Tiberius Caesar, ..." This verse is making reference to John the Baptist and when he began his ministry. Since Jesus is six months younger that John, Tiberius could have been in his 16th year of reign when Jesus began His ministry.

Africanus ends his work on chronology with this statement. "The period, then, to the advent of the Lord from Adam and the creation is 5531 years, from which epoch to the 250th Olympiad there are 192 years, as has been shown above." I believe that he is saying from creation to the advent of our Lord is 5531 years, and this epoch ends 192 years before the 250th Olympiad. Jesus then began His ministry in A.D. 29. This is not the year that He was born, as we might infer from the word 'advent'. The start of the Christian era, according to Africanus' chronology, would be 5531—29 = 5502 A.M.

In summarizing, the time intervals calculated by Africanus are: creation of Adam—2262 years—Flood—940 years—Abraham's birth—361 years—death of Joseph—???—Exodus—1237 years—Cyrus became king of Persia—115 years—Artaxerxes' command to rebuild Jerusalem—475 years—Christ began His Ministry = 5531 years (A.D. 29). See Figure 2. The writings of Africanus failed to include the interval between the death of Joseph and the Exodus. We can calculate that interval of time by subtracting the subtotal from 5531 years to get 141 years. [I calculate this time interval to be 154 years. See Figure 3: Chronology of Biblical Events in <u>The 7th Millennium</u> document for the dates of these two events.]

Chronological Event	Africanus' calculations-years	My calculations-years
Creation to Flood	2262	1656
Flood to Abraham's birth	940	352
Abraham's birth to Joseph's death	361	361
Joseph's death to Exodus	141	154
Exodus to Cyrus' reign	1237	910
Cyrus' reign to Command to rebuild Jerusalem	115	95
Jerusalem rebuilt to Christ's begins His Ministry	475	472
<<<<<<<<Total years from creation to A.D. 29	5531	4000

Figure 2

Conclusion

1. Africanus probably used a version of the Septuagint for his Biblical source reference. The version he used could not be found. The Septuagint gave him a much older earth than the Hebrew text because the age of the patriarchs when they propagated their successor was usually 100 years larger.

2. His omission of Cainan as one of the post-diluvian progenitors of Christ would tend to support the Hebrew text in this area. Josephus and the writers of the Samaritan Pentateuch also omitted Cainan.

3. Africanus' interpretation of Daniel's '70 weeks' contradicts Scripture. He should have used 69 weeks of years rather than 70 weeks of years. He also defined a year as being a lunar year, or 354 days. A year is defined (by inference reasoning: 1260 days = 42 months = 3 1/2 years) as 360 days in the book of Revelation.

References

1) The New Encyclopaedia Britannica, Volume 1, page 136.
2) The Extant Writings of Julius Africanus, These writings of Africanus can be obtained off of the internet at <http://www.newadvent.org/fathers/0614.htm>.
3) Antiquities of the Jews, b.1, c.6, s.4. The Works of Flavius Josephus, translated by William Whiston, Baker Book House, 1975.
4) Persia and the Bible, Edwin M. Yamauchi, pages 72—92, Baker Book House, 1990.

CHAPTER 7

DATING CHRIST'S DEATH AND RESURRECTION

Reference: New King James Version of the Bible

Background

The day, as we think of it, starts at 12:00 o'clock midnight and runs to the following 12:00 o'clock midnight. The Jewish day starts approx. 6 hours earlier than our day; i.e., at sundown and runs until sundown the following day. Since Christ's resurrection occurred shortly after the vernal equinox, sundown was approx. at 6:00 o'clock PM and sunrise was approx. at 6:00 o'clock AM. The Jewish night time and day time were from sundown until sunrise and from sunrise until sundown, respectfully. Our night time and day time are the same as the Jews.

The <u>Jewish calendar</u> is based on the lunar cycle along with the solar cycle. The Jewish year consists of 12 or 13 lunar months. They are: 1) Nisan, 2) Iyyar, 3) Sivan, 4) Tammuz, 5) Av, 6) Elul, 7) Tishri, 8) Heshvan, 9) Kislev, 10) Tevet, 11) Shevat, 12) Adar I and sometimes 13) <u>Adar II</u>. Every month has its beginning when the moon is in conjunction with the sun, or another way of saying it, when the moon goes through the New Moon phase. The Jewish ceremonial year begins with the Nisan New Moon which occurs around the Spring or Vernal Equinox. Adar II is added after Adar I seven times in a nineteen-year cycle to keep the lunar time period approximately equal to the solar time period. The mean synodic month, called a lunation, is 29 days, 12 hours, 44 minutes, and 2.8 seconds. The 1900 solar or <u>tropical year</u> is 365 days, 5 hours, 48 minutes, and 46 seconds. $((19\times12)+7) \times 29.530588 = 6939.68818$ is approximately equal to $19 \times 365.24220 = 6939.6018$. Therefore, the lunar time period exceeds the solar time period by less than a day in 200 years.

Christ's resurrection was on Sunday morning, either before sunrise or shortly after sunrise.

Matthew 28:1,2

1) **Now after the Sabbath, as the first day of the week began to dawn, Mary Magdalene and the other Mary came to see the tomb.**

2) **And behold, there was a great earthquake; for an angel of the Lord descended from heaven, and came and rolled back the stone from the door, and sat on it.**

<u>Mark 16:1—4</u>

1) **Now when the Sabbath was past, Mary Magdalene, Mary the mother of James, and Salome bought spices, that they might come and anoint Him.**

2) **Very early in the morning, on the first day of the week, they came to the tomb when the sun had risen.**

3) **And they said among themselves, "Who will roll away the stone from the door of the tomb for us?"**

4) **But when they looked up, they saw that the stone had been rolled away—for it was very large.** [These passages leave the door open for a possibility of the resurrection occurring very shortly after sunrise. In any case, Christ's resurrection on the Sunday, first day of the week.]

Luke 24:1,2

1) **Now on the first day of the week, very early in the morning, they, and certain other women with them came to the tomb bringing the spices which they had prepared.**

2) **But they found the stone rolled away from the tomb.**

John 20:1

1) **On the first day of the week Mary Magdalene came to the tomb early, while it was still dark, and saw that the stone had been taken away from the tomb.** [This would indicate that the resurrection had already occurred when it was still night or before the sun was up.]

Jesus was in the heart of the earth three days and three nights.

Matthew 12:40

40) **"For as Jonah was three days and three nights in the belly of the great fish, so will the Son of Man be three days and three nights in the heart of the earth."** [Spoken by Jesus.]

Jonah 1:17

17) **Now the Lord had prepared a great fish to swallow Jonah. And Jonah was in the belly of the fish three days and three nights.**

Sabbaths were a day of solemn rest, a holy convocation, where the Israelites were commanded by God to do no customary work.

The seventh day of the week is a Sabbath.

Leviticus 23:3

3) **Six days shall work be done, but the seventh day is a Sabbath of solemn rest, a holy convocation. You shall do no work on it; it is the Sabbath of the Lord in all your dwellings.**

The Feast of Unleavened Bread is a Sabbath.

Leviticus 23:5—8

5) **On the fourteenth day of the first month at twilight is the Lord's Passover.** [Passover starts with the killing of the lamb at the end of Nisan 14. Nisan 14 is not a day of solemn rest. It was called the Day of Preparation. The Jews were to kill the Passover lamb late in the

day time—"at twilight" or evening is about the ninth hour or 3:00 o'clock PM and before sunset.]

6) **And on the fifteenth day of the same month is the Feast of Unleavened Bread to the Lord; seven days you must eat unleavened bread.** [Nisan 15—21]

7) **On the first day you shall have a holy convocation; you shall do no customary work on it.** [Nisan 15]

8) **But you shall offer an offering made by fire to the Lord for seven days. The seventh day shall be a holy convocation; you shall do no customary work on it.** [Nisan 21]

Day of Preparation (<u>Nisan 14</u>) is the day the Jews were to purge their home of all leaven.

<u>Matthew 27:62</u>, 63
62) **On the next day, which followed the Day of Preparation, the chief priests and Pharisees gathered together to Pilate,**

63) **saying, "Sir, we remember, while He was still alive, how that deceiver said, 'After three days I will rise.'**

Mark 15:42
42) **Now when evening had come, because it was the Preparation Day, that is, the day before the Sabbath,** [Evening or twilight had already come and it still was Nisan 14.]

Luke 23:53, 54
53) **Then he took it down, wrapped it in linen, and laid it in a tomb that was hewn out of the rock, where no one had ever lain before.**

54) **That day was the Preparation, and the Sabbath drew near.** [The phrase 'the Sabbath drew near' could be referring to the <u>Feast of Unleavened Bread</u>, or to the seventh day of the week, or to both.]

John 19:14
14) **Now it was the Preparation Day of the Passover, and about the sixth hour. And he said to the Jews, "Behold your King!"** [Pilate said this about noon on Nisan 14.]

John 19:31
31) **Therefore, because it was the Preparation, that the bodies should not remain on the cross on the Sabbath (for that Sabbath was a high day), the Jews asked Pilate that their legs might be broken, and that they might be taken away.** ['that Sabbath was a high day' could mean the Feast of Unleavened Bread is a high day, or that the seventh day of the week is a high day, or simply a Sabbath period which is 48 hours long.]

John 19:42
42) **So there they laid Jesus, because of the Jews' Preparation Day, for the tomb was nearby.**

Assuming that Christ was in the tomb for three days and three nights, the calculations are as follows:

Day 1	Nisan 14 about 3:00 PM	Christ died on the cross on Preparation Day
Night 1	Nisan 15	Jews celebrating the Feast of Unleavened Bread
Day 2	Nisan 15	The Feast of Unleavened Bread (day time hours)
Night 2	Nisan 16	Seventh <u>day of week</u> begins (night time hours)
Day 3	Nisan 16	The daylight hours of the seventh day of week
Night 3	Nisan 17 just before sunrise	Christ was raised on the first day of the week during the night time hours
3 days & 3 nights; a period of approx. 63 hours		

What year was Christ's death? Since this question has not been answered definitively, a period of 10 years will be looked at—from A.D. 27 to A.D. 36.

Nisan is the first month of the Jewish ceremonial calendar and is determined by the Vernal (Spring) Equinox. The Vernal Equinox and the Nisan New Moon phase were calculated using <u>Astronomical Tables of the Sun, Moon, and Planets</u> by Jean Meeus and published by Willmann-Bell, Inc. These are provided in a table (columns 2 and 3) below. The time is given in h for hours and in m for minutes. UT is Universal Time or Greenwich Mean Time (GMT) and JT is Jerusalem Time. Since Jerusalem time is two hours ahead of Greenwich, England, the Jewish day starts approx. 8 hours earlier than Universal Time. Therefore, any UT greater than 16 h would be the next day in Jerusalem by the Jews method of logging days.

The 4th column is the start (6 PM) of the Day of Preparation which is Nisan 14. This would be about the time, or a few hours later, when Jesus and his disciples celebrated the Passover meal, better known as the Lord's Supper. They celebrated the Passover meal the evening before the rest of the Jews celebrated it.

Year —A.D.	Vernal Equinox (date, day, time—UT)	Nisan New Moon (date, day, time—UT)	Start of Preparation Day—Nisan 14 @ 6 PM (date, day @ 6 PM—JT)
27	Mar. 23, Sun., 5h, 15m	Mar. 26, Wed., 17h, 57m	Apr. 9, Wednesday
28	Mar. 22, Mon., 11h, 3m	Mar. 15, Mon., 0h, 26m	Mar. 28, Sunday
29	Mar. 22, Tue., 16h, 52m	Apr. 2, Sat., 17h, 22m	Apr. 16, Saturday
30	Mar. 22, Wed., 22h, 41m	Mar. 22, Wed., 17h, 42m	Apr. 5, Wednesday
31	Mar. 23, Fri., 4h, 30m	Apr. 10, Tue., 11h, 30m	Apr. 23, Monday
32	Mar. 22, Sat., 10h, 19m	Mar. 29, Sat., 20h, 1m	Apr. 12, Saturday
33	Mar. 22, Sun., 16h, 8m	Mar. 19, Thu., 10h, 37m	Apr. 1, Wednesday
34	Mar. 22, Mon., 21h, 57m	Apr. 7, Wed., 11h, 42m	Apr. 20, Tuesday
35	Mar. 23, Wed., 3h, 45m	Mar. 28, Mon., 4h, 2m	Apr. 10, Sunday
36	Mar. 22, Thu., 9h, 34m	Mar. 16, Fri., 15h, 46m	Mar. 30, Friday

From this table you can see there are only 3 years (A.D. 27, 30, and 33) that the crucifixion could have occurred on Thursday. Luke 3:1 would rule out A.D. 27 on the basis of being too early.

Luke 3:1
1) **Now in the fifteenth year of the reign of Tiberius Caesar, Pontius Pilate being governor of Judea, Herod being tetrarch of Galilee, his brother Philip tetrarch of <u>Iturea</u> and the region of Trachonitis, and <u>Lysanias</u> tetrarch of Abilene, . . .**

The phrase 'in the fifteenth year of the reign of Tiberius Caesar' is the beginning of John the Baptist ministry. John was 6 months older than Jesus. John had to be at least 30 years old to enter the service of the Lord (Num. 4:3). So, John had already been baptizing people for at least 6 months when Jesus' began His ministry. For simplicity, assume it is still during the fifteenth year of the reign of Tiberius Caesar when Jesus began His ministry.

Tiberius Caesar's reign began August 19, A.D. 14. (Re: 15th edition of Britannia, Vol. 11, p. 755) Pontius Pilate reigned for 10 years from A.D. 26 to A.D. 36. The fifteenth year of the reign of Tiberius Caesar was between August 19, A.D. 28 and August 19, A.D. 29. Therefore, Jesus' crucifixion would have had to occur in A.D. 30 or A.D. 33. Unlike the Babylonians, the regal year for the Grecian and Roman governments began when they took the throne. The regal year of the Babylonians started the following Nisan 1.

Partial Conclusion:
The conjunction of the moon with the sun for the start of Nisan in A.D. 30 occurred at 5:42 p.m. on March 22 UT, but because Jerusalem was two hours ahead of England's time it was too late to start Nisan that evening. The conjunction occurs at 12:37 p.m. Jerusalem Time in A.D. 33, so Nisan 1 would have started that evening. Nisan 14 would be the Preparation Day, and it would have started the day before on Wednesday evening around 6 o'clock. Jesus' death was either on Thursday, April 6, A.D. 30 or Thursday, April 2, A.D. 33 at approximately 3 PM Jerusalem time. And Jesus' resurrection was either on Sunday, April 9, A.D. 30 or Sunday, April 5, A.D. 33 just before sunrise.

How many years was Jesus' ministry on earth? Even though tradition tells us that his ministry was three and a half years, it is only, at best, an educated estimate. It could have been as short as a little over two years by John's gospel, if it started February 19, A.D. 29, or as much as five years.

The gospel according to John is the only book that one can deduce a minimum time period for His ministry. There are at least three separate Passovers that Jesus attended. They are as follows:

<u>Passover 1—John 2</u>
Verses 1-12 is traditionally Jesus' first miracle—changing water into wine at the wedding of Cana.

Verses 13-7 tell of Jesus cleansing the Temple. (the Passover was at hand)

Verses 18-22 tell of Jesus foretelling his death and resurrection.

19) **Jesus answered and said to them, "Destroy this temple, and in three days I will raise it up."**

20) **Then the Jews said, "It has taken forty-six years to build this temple, and you will raise it up in three days?"**

The phrase **'forty-six years to build this temple'** can be used to approximate the year when Herod the Great began his reign. Josephus tells us in his 15th Book, Chapter 11, Section 1 of the Antiquities of the Jews that Herod started remodeling the temple in the eighteenth year of his reign. If Josephus and the Jews who said this are correct, then Herod began his reign in 36 B.C. Most historians state that Herod began his reign in 37 B.C.

Verses 23—25 is where Jesus was in Jerusalem at the Passover.

Passover 2—John 6
Verses 1—14 is the narrative telling of feeding five thousand with five barley loaves and two small fish by the Sea of Galilee.

4) **Now the Passover, a feast of the Jews, was near.** In John 7:2 the Feast of Tabernacles was near, and in John 10:22 it was the Feast of Dedication.

Passover 3—John 12—19
John 12:1 to John 19:42 tells of the activity around the Passover at which Jesus was crucified.

This would make the date of Jesus' death, as a minimum, A.D. 31.

Conclusion:
The gospel according to John tends to rule out A.D. 30 as the year of Christ's death and resurrection. The year A.D. 30 could only be the year of Christ's death and resurrection if Tiberius Caesar began his reign in A.D. 13 instead of 14. It is unlikely that historians are wrong about this date.

The following is additional supportive evidence that Jesus' death and resurrection occurred in A.D. 33.

Daniel 9:24—27

24) **"Seventy weeks are determined** **For your people and for your holy city,** **To finish the transgression,** **To make an end of sins,** **To make reconciliation for iniquity,** **To bring in everlasting righteousness,** **To seal up vision and prophecy,** **And to anoint the Most Holy.**	[70 weeks of years or 490 years; 1 week of years = 1 * 7 * 360 days]
25) **"Know therefore and understand,** **That from the going forth of the command** **To restore and build Jerusalem** **Until Messiah the Prince,** **There shall be seven weeks and sixty-two weeks;** **The street shall be built again, and the wall,** **Even in troublesome times.**	[For the command to restore and build Jerusalem see Nehemiah 1:1 to 2:10] [7 * 7 years and 62 * 7 years]
26) **"And after the sixty-two weeks** **Messiah shall be cut off, but not for Himself;** **And the people of the prince who is to come** **Shall destroy the city and the sanctuary.** **The end of it shall be with a flood,** **And till the end of the war desolations are determined.**	[the prince = Titus]
27) **"Then he shall confirm a covenant with many for a week;** **But in the middle of the week** **He shall bring an end to sacrifice and offering.** **And on the wing of abominations shall be one who makes desolate,** **Even until the consummation which is determined,** **Is poured out on the desolate."**	[he = antichrist & 1 * 7 years] [1 * 3 1/2 years = 42 months = 1260 days re: Rev. 11:2,3 & 12:6]

What is the definition of 70 weeks? The 70 weeks are divided up into 7 weeks + 62 weeks + 1 week. Then the one week spoken of in verse 27 is broken down into two equal parts of one-half week where it says, **"But in the middle of the week"**. This is what is known as the Great Tribulation spoken of in the Old and New Testament. In Rev. 12:6, it is said to be 1260 days. In Rev. 12:14, it is said to be a time and times and half a time or 3 1/2 years and in Rev. 13:5, it is said to be 42 months. 1260 days = 42 months of 30 days per month = 3 1/2 years of 360 days per year. Therefore, 2520 days = 84 months of 30 days per month = 7 years of 360 days per year = 1 week. And, 70 weeks = 490 years of 360 days/year = 5880 months of 30 days/month = 176,400 days. Thus, Sixty-nine weeks = 173,880 days. [A 30-day month and a 360 day-year appear to be the length of a month and year at the time of the Noahic flood. The flood began on the 17th day of the second month (Gen. 7:11). The waters prevailed on the earth for 150 days (Gen. 7:24 and 8:3). The ark came to rest on Mount Ararat on the 17th day of the seventh month (Gen. 8:4). Five months of 30 days/month = 150 days.]

Nehemiah 2:1 says that it was the month of Nisan in the twentieth year of King Artaxerxes.

Nehemiah 2:8 says that King Artaxerxes granted Nehemiah's wish to rebuild Jerusalem.

Artaxerxes began his reign April 13, 464 B.C. so his 20th year is between April 13, 445 B.C. and April 13, 444 B.C. [Re: <u>Persia and the Bible</u> by Edwin M. Yamauchi, page 248.]

The Julian Calendar was adopted in 44 B.C. under the reign of Julius Caesar. Prior to 44 B.C. the Romans had what is called today the original Roman calendar which consisted of 10 months or a total of 304 days. In 444 B.C. the Jews were under the control of Medo-Persian rule anyway. And after 332 B.C. they were under Grecian control. So that is why the calculations that follow use an Julian Calendar Equivalent (JCE). It shouldn't make any difference if we do not care what <u>Persian calendar</u> date it falls on as long as the lunar cycle and the <u>tropical year</u> are predictable. The Nisan New Moon occurred on March 4, 444 B.C. JCE.

28 days	Mar. 4, 444 B.C. to Mar. 31, 444 B.C. inclusive
275 days	Apr. 1, 444 B.C. to Dec. 31, 444 B.C. inclusive
161,806 days	Jan. 1, 443 B.C. to Dec. 31, 1 B.C. inclusive
11,688 days	Jan. 1, A.D. 1 to Dec. 31, A.D. 32 inclusive
92 days	Jan. 1, A.D. 33 to Apr. 2, A.D. 33 (Nisan 14) inclusive
173,889 days	Total days between Mar. 4, 444 B.C. and Apr. 2, A.D. 33

The 173,889 days is nine days more than (7 * 7 + 62 * 7) * 360 or 173,880 days spoken of in Daniel. Nisan 1, 444 B.C. to Nisan 14, A.D. 33 inclusive is 173,889 days. We don't know the exact date when the prophecy was given during the month of Nisan. If the prophecy was given on Nisan 10, 444 B.C., it would be exactly 173,880 days before Jesus was crucified.

The prophecy in Daniel also answers another question I have had for some time. How could the wise men from the East know when the right time was for the Messiah to be born (Matthew 2:1,2) if they didn't see the prophecy in Daniel 9:24—27? There are no other passages in the Old Testament which tell when the Messiah was to be born. This prophecy would give the wise men a 'ball park' period of time for the Messiah's birth.

Other dates suggested for the death and resurrection of Christ:
1. The year A.D. 32 has been suggested.

1a. Preparation Day (Nisan 14) for A.D. 32 is on a Saturday. But because it would be on the Sabbath, Preparation Day would have been postponed one day until Sunday. Therefore, the Feast of Unleavened Bread, or Nisan 15, would be on Monday. But, we know that Christ rose on Sunday, the first day of the week.

2. A Wednesday crucifixion with a Sunday resurrection has been suggested.

2a. God says that His Holy One will not see corruption (Ps. 16:10, Acts 2:27). Again, scripture is true and infallible. Lazarus was dead four days and stinking when Jesus raised him (John 11:39). People being dead for four days are decaying.

2b. A Wednesday crucifixion would mean that Thursday was a Sabbath, the Feast of Unleavened Bread, and Friday was not a Sabbath. It means that the woman could have gone to the tomb on Friday, a non-Sabbath, to anoint Jesus' body. But the proponents of a Wednesday crucifixion say that the women would be unclean and couldn't worship in the temple the next day, the weekly Sabbath. This is true. The argument falls apart though. Anyone that touches a dead body is unclean for a period seven days. So the women would have had to miss one weekly Sabbath, including the Sabbath on Nisan 21, because of the Jewish Law of Purification (Num. 19:11).

3. People have suggested that at the time of the crucifixion, the Jews had to see the New Moon to declare it to be the first of the month. So, if it was cloudy for 5 days in Palestine during the time of the conjunction, the month wouldn't start until the 6th day.

3a. Even if a person would accept a delay in starting the month, it doesn't necessarily mean that those feast days during the month would also be delayed. I believe the Jews calculated the time of the conjunction similar to the way they do it today.

4. People have suggested that the Jews perform an intercalation of the New Moon exactly as they do today, i.e., Rosh Ha Shanah (Tishri 1) is never allowed to fall on a Sunday, Wednesday or Friday due to the way the Jews do their intercalation. (Vol. 5, p 44 of Encyclopedia Judaica)

4a. Present intercalation was put into practice under Hillel II, who lived during the 4th century of the Christian era. In fact, the present intercalation was not yet established during the 11th century of the Christian era. Quoting from the Encyclopedia Judaica, Vol. 5, p. 50, "There is, on the other hand, unimpeachable evidence from the works of writers with expert knowledge of the calendar that the present ordo intercalations and epochal molad were not yet intrinsic parts of the calendar of Hillel II, these being seen still side by side with other styles of ordo intercalationis and the molad as late as the 11 century." The Jews went through several versions of adjusting their calendar, but never more than one day at the most. Even if the calendar was adjusted by a day, A.D. 31 and 32, the two most likely candidates, would not qualify.

I would be amiss if I did not tell you of another possibility. This possibility has to do with the way we interpret Scripture.

Jesus said, **"For as Jonah was three days and three nights in the belly of the great fish, so will the Son of Man be three days and three nights in the heart of the earth."** (Matt. 12:40.) Most people think of Christ as being dead when they apply the three days and three nights, but what if it included His suffering and crucifixion also? What if the time mentioned in Matt. 12:40 was to start after the Passover Meal (the Lord's Supper) when Jesus was in the Garden of Gethsemane praying? Do we have Bible passages that lead us to believe this is the case? Maybe.

Matthew 26:36-38
Then Jesus came with them to a place called Gethsemane, and said to the disciples, "Sit here while I go and pray over there." And He took with Him Peter and the two sons of

Zebedee, and <u>He began to be sorrowful and deeply distressed</u>. "My soul is exceedingly sorrowful, even to death. Stay here and watch with Me."

Mark 14:32-34
Then they came to a place which was named Gethsemane; and He said to His disciples, "Sit here while I pray." And He took Peter, James, and John with Him, and <u>He began to be troubled and deeply distressed</u>. Then He said to them, "My soul is exceedingly sorrowful, even to death. Stay here and watch."

Luke and John give no time when Jesus anguish started like Matthew and Mark. However, John records that Jesus gave His disciples a 'pep talk' in chapters 14 through 17. In chapter 17 verse 1 Jesus prays for Himself when He said, **"Father, <u>the hour has come</u>. Glorify Your Son, that Your Son also may glorify You."**

The underlined words in these three passages seem to support the concept that Jesus was abandoned by God during His suffering in the <u>garden of Gethsemane</u> the night before His crucifixion. Luke records Jesus agony as being so intense that His sweat became like great drops of blood falling down to the ground (Luke 22:44). During His crucifixion we know that Jesus was abandoned when He cried out with a loud voice, saying, **"My God, My God, why have You forsaken Me?"** (Matt. 27:46 and Mark 15:34)

So, it is possible to conclude that Jesus was in the bowels of the earth, cut-off from God, even before His death.

Now if we assume a Thursday night arrest, a Friday trial and crucifixion, and a Sunday morning resurrection we will get the three nights and three days that Jesus prophesied.

Night 1	Nisan 14 about 10:00 PM	Christ started to suffer the night before His death
Day 1	Nisan 14	Christ trial, crucifixion, & death (Preparation Day)
Night 2	Nisan 15	The Feast of Unleavened Bread (Passover Meal)
Day 2	Nisan 15	The Feast of Unleavened Bread (daytime hours)
Night 3	Nisan 16	The night time hours following the Sabbath
Day 3	Nisan 16 just after sunrise	Christ was raised on the first day of the week during the day time hours
3 nights & 3 days; a period of approx. 56 hours		

A Friday crucifixion however would mean that the New Moon for the month of Nisan had to occur after sundown in Jerusalem on Thursday, or for some other reason, Nisan 1 was delayed a day. The idea that the sun and moon conjunction calculation is in error is most unlikely. But, it is possible that Nisan 1 was delayed one day. The Jews were possibly using an <u>intercalation</u> process, different, but not too dissimilar from the one they are using today. The calendar for Nisan for the year A.D. 33 would start on Saturday rather than on Friday thereby making Nisan 14 (Preparation Day) fall on Friday.

The prophecy in Daniel still works if we adjust our thinking. The New Moon on Nisan 1, 444 B.C. JCE has to be delayed by a day just as it had to be for A.D. 33. The reason for postponing the establishment of Nisan 1 is unknown, but whatever the reason was for delaying it one day in A.D. 33 is also applied to the start of Nisan 1, 444 B.C.

27 days	Mar. 5, 444 B.C. to Mar. 31, 444 B.C. inclusive
275 days	Apr. 1, 444 B.C. to Dec. 31, 444 B.C. inclusive
161,806 days	Jan. 1, 443 B.C. to Dec. 31, 1 B.C. inclusive
11,688 days	Jan. 1, A.D. 1 to Dec. 31, A.D. 32 inclusive
93 days	Jan. 1, A.D. 33 to Apr. 3, A.D. 33 (Nisan 14) inclusive
173,889 days	Total days between Mar. 5, 444 B.C. and Apr. 3, A.D. 33

The total number of days is still 173,889, if we lower the top entry to 27 days and increase the bottom entry to 93 days.

Now, supposing that Jesus' crucifixion and death did occur on Friday, the sixth day of the week. What ramifications, if any, does this have on the way we interpret or understand Scriptures?

Genesis 2:17 the Lord said, "... **for in the day that you eat of it you shall surely die.**" Adam did die spiritually the same day that he did eat. But, he did not die physically until hundreds of years later. But it could also mean 'in the day of the week' that you eat, you shall surely die, as some of the early Christians, such as, Ireneaus of Lyons (c.130—c.200) believed? See Ireneaus Against Heresies, Book V, Chapter XXIII. This reference can be obtained on the Internet at <http://www.ccel.org/fathers2/ANF-01/anf01-63.htm#TopOfPage>.

Quoting Ireneaus, "From this it is clear that the Lord suffered death, in obedience to His Father, upon that day on which Adam died while he disobeyed God. Now he died on the same day in which he did eat. For God said, "In that day on which ye shall eat of it, ye shall die by death." The Lord, therefore, recapitulating in Himself this day, underwent His sufferings upon the day preceding the Sabbath, that is, the sixth day of the creation, on which day man was created; thus granting him a second creation by means of His passion, which is that [creation] out of death."

Ireneaus believed that Adam ate of the forbidden fruit on the sixth day, the same day that he and Eve were created by God. Likewise the New Adam, Christ, was crucified and died on the sixth day of the week, rested on the Sabbath, and rose on the eighth day or the first day of a new week.

The sixth day is man's day, just as the number 6 is man's number. Man took it upon himself to disobey God and brought sin into the world. Ever since man has been disobeying God by not putting Him first, by not loving God, by not keeping the Sabbath Day holy. Christ's died on man's day. The New Adam died on man's day and rested on the Sabbath. Christ kept the Sabbath for us as He did all of the commandments. Christ arose to take us into a new week and into eternity. Christ is like the phoenix bird arising out of the ashes of mankind, giving us a new beginning.

Conclusion
Jesus was crucified on Thursday, April 2 or Friday, April 3, A.D. 33 and rose again on Sunday, April 5, A.D. 33. [There was a partial lunar eclipse after sundown on Friday, April 3, A.D. 33 in Jerusalem.] There is some doubt about these dates, but there is no doubt about what I am going to say now. Jesus was crucified and died because of my sins and your sins. Three days later God raised Jesus from the dead. Jesus offers me, and everyone else, the free gift of eternal life if we believe this. Lord Jesus, I believe.

CHAPTER 8
AN UNDERSTANDING OF ESCHATOLOGY

No one knows the Day or Hour

Matthew 24:36-44 and Luke 17:20-37 tell us: **Then two men will be in the field: one will be taken and the other left. Two women will be grinding at the mill: one will be taken and the other left.**

Question 1: Is it the saved or the unsaved which will be taken?

Those who believe it is the saved people that are taken argue that Noah left in an ark (Matthew 24:36-44) and Lot walked out of Sodom (Luke 17:20-37).

Those who believe it is the unsaved people that are taken argue that the wicked ones were taken out of this world by God in the days of Noah and Lot.

Question 2: When is this talking about?

The millennialists say at the rapture. Some say at the beginning of the tribulation period. Some say at the midpoint of the tribulation and some say at the end of the tribulation at Christ's second coming. Some probably even say at the end of the 1000-year reign of Christ? The amillennialists say at the end of the world or age, and there is only one age and it has its end at the end of the world.

The Parable of the Wise and Foolish Virgins (Matthew 25:1-13)

Marriage of Jesus Christ and the Church tells us the ten virgins went out to meet Christ. The five foolish virgins did not have any oil for their lamps, so they went to buy some. The five wise virgins went in with the bridegroom to the wedding. The five foolish virgins came back and tried to get in, but the door was shut.

Question 1: What or Who are the virgins?

The visible church.

Question 2: Who are the wise virgins?

The believing people. Those baptized by Christ. The born-again people. The Christians.

Question 3: Who are the foolish virgins?

The people who say they are Christian, but aren't. They are christians who have not been baptized by Christ. Those who are carnal christians.

Question 4: Why are they called virgins?

They are called virgins because they are referred to by people of the world as Christians. Definition: wise virgins = Christians; foolish virgins = christians with a small 'c'.

The Parable of the Faithful Servant and the Evil Servant (Luke 12:35-48)

In verse 35, the servants are warned to be ready to eat (**having your waist be girded**) and with faith (**your lamps burning**). In verse 36 the servants are to watch and wait for their Lord for **when He returns from the wedding**, He will knock and they should open the door immediately. In verse 37, the Lord will gird Himself (preparing to eat) and have the servants sit down to eat and the Lord will serve them.

In these verses our Lord has been to a wedding. I believe the wedding is our wedding—Christ and the Church.

And I believe we will have the wedding ceremony when we are raptured. In the rapture, the saved people will be taken and the unsaved will be left as stated in the parable about ten virgins.

In studying Romans 11:21-24, the Jews, as a nation, are going to get another chance to come to know Christ. They will be grafted back into the olive tree, from which they were cut-off. The natural branches will be grafted back on the olive tree where the wild branches (that is us Gentiles) were grafted.

We would be wise not to think of those missing the rapture as being given a 'second chance'. Although, all of us Christians have had many second chances. As II Thessalonians 2:1-12 says, **"God will send them a strong delusion, that they should believe the lie"**. I believe it will be just as hard, or harder, for the Gentiles, at least those christian Gentiles, to believe after the rapture as it was for the Jews during the last 2000 years. Remember, when Christ cursed the barren fig tree it died immediately. See Matthew 21:18-22 and Mark 11:12-14, 20-24. Life has not been good for the Jewish nation these past two millennia.

The Old Testament has some references to Israel 'getting a second chance'. In Amos 9:14-15 it says, **"I will bring back the captives of My people Israel; they shall build the waste cities and inhabit them, they shall plant vineyards and drink wine from them; they shall also make gardens and eat fruit from them. I will plant them in their land, and no longer shall they be pulled up from the land I have given them."** Says the Lord your God.'

Jeremiah 31:36 describes it this way. **"If those ordinances** [i.e., the ordinance of the sun providing light by day, the moon and stars light by night] **depart from before Me,"** says the Lord, **"Then the seed of Israel shall also cease from being a nation before Me forever."** My pastor during my early teen years when I was taking instruction for confirming my faith (I got confirmed in 1947) said that the Israel talked about in these passages was the 'new Israel', that is, the Christians. I didn't know whether I believed it then but I don't believe it now.

Romans 11:26 says, **"And so all Israel will be saved, as it is written** (in Isaiah 59:20-21)**: The Deliverer will come out of Zion, and He will turn away ungodliness from Jacob; for this is My covenant with them, when I take away their sins."**

So, is it so hard to believe that there will be 144,000 Jewish evangelists during the tribulation period as stated in Revelation 7? I think not.

Near the end of the <u>great tribulation</u> Christ will make His appearance on earth. This is referred to as His Second Coming by both the millennialists and non-millennialists (<u>amillennialists</u>). The world will be purged of all non-Christians at this time. The unsaved people will be taken at that time. The world will consists of only people who believe in Jesus Christ. All Israel will be saved. Just as in the days of Noah, all believers were saved. They will go into the millennial reign of Christ.

During the millennial reign of Christ a great deal of Scripture will be fulfilled literally, such as, Isaiah 65:17-25, Isaiah 66:14-24, Ezekiel 40-48, Zechariah 14:16-20, and Revelation 20 where the 1000 years are referred to six different times.

Neither do you have a contradiction of Ezekiel 29:8-16 with Christianity's teaching of an imminent return of Christ. Verse 11 says, **"that neither foot of man shall pass through it nor foot of beast pass through it, and it shall be uninhabited forty years"**. It here is Egypt. This prophecy has not been fulfilled yet. I am expecting the literal fulfillment of this prophecy sometime in the future, possibly during the tribulation and millennial reign of Jesus Christ.

An amillennialist would have to say this prophecy has been fulfilled symbolically, or has yet to be fulfilled. If it is yet to be fulfilled it means that Christ's return is not, and never was, imminent.

Christ reigns with an iron hand during His millennial reign. Satan is put in prison at Christ's Second Coming. Mankind doesn't need any prodding by the king of liars. 'We can do it all by ourselves'.

At the end of the 1000 years, Satan is released from prison and goes out to deceive the nations on the earth. A great battle ensues between Jesus Christ and His enemies. Jesus Christ wins the war. Court convenes. This is called the <u>great white throne judgment</u> in the <u>book of Revelation</u>. The unsaved are sent to the lake of fire.

The saved go with Jesus Christ to the new Jerusalem which is heaven. There is no sun, no moon, no night, no time, no sea, and no temple in the city. Heaven is full of the Light of the Christ.

Other passages in the Tanach (Old Testament), than the ones already mentioned, which refer to:

1. the remnant of Israel—Is 10:21-23, Is 11:10-16, Is 41:9, Is 43:6, Is 44:21, Is 49:15, Je 30:11, Je 31:36-37, Ez 37-39, Ho 6:2, Am 8:2, Mi 2:12, Zp 3:13.

2. the rapture—Ps 12:1, Ps 27:5, Ps 47:5, Ps 81:3, Is 18:3-6, Is 26:19-21, Is 57:1, Jl 2:1, Mi 7:2, Zp 2:3

3. the tribulation period—Ps 27:5, Is 2:5-19, Is 13, Is 24:1-20, Is 26:1-19, Is 27:12-13, Is 60:2, Je 30:7, Ez 32:6-16, Jl 2:15-16, Jl 3:9-10

4. the millennial period—Ps 2:9, Is 2:1-4, Is 4, Is 11:3-16, Is 24:21-23, Is 35:5-10

5. the saints reign with Jesus during the millennial period—Ps 149:5-9

6. heaven for the remnant of Israel—Is 60:19-22

CHAPTER 9

PASSAGES SUPPORTING A 6000-YEAR EARTH
AND
A MILLENNIAL REIGN OF CHRIST

1.   <u>One thousand years = One day</u>

Gen. 2:17 reads, **"but of the tree of the knowledge of good and evil you shall not eat, for in the day that you eat of it you shall surely die."** Adam died when he was 930 years old, so God's word was held true, for Adam died in the <u>day</u> that he did eat.

Psalm 90:4 reads, **"For a thousand years in Your sight Are like yesterday when it is past, And like a watch in the night."**

II Peter 3:8 reads, **"But, beloved, do not forget this one thing, that with the Lord one day is as a thousand years, and a thousand years as one day."**

2.   <u>Church Age = 2 days or 2000 years???</u>

John 2:1 reads, **"<u>On the third day</u> there was a wedding in Cana of Galilee . . ."** which infers that there was two days prior to this day. This reminds us of the heavenly wedding that the church is going to experience when the bridegroom, Jesus Christ, takes the church for His bride. The two days prior to the third day is the 2000 years of the church age. [See Jewish Wedding below for details.]

John 4:43 reads, **"Now <u>after the two days</u> He** (Jesus) **departed from there** (Samaria) **and went to Galilee."** Jesus spent two days with the Samaritans, a Gentile nation, which received Him and His teachings. So, also He has spent 2000 years with the Gentile nations, saving them and witnessing to them.

Luke 13:32 reads, **"And He** (Jesus) **said to them, Go, tell that fox** (Herod), **'Behold, I cast out demons and perform cures <u>today</u> and <u>tomorrow</u>, and <u>the third day</u> I shall be perfected.'"** Jesus prophesied that there will be 2000 years between His First Coming and His Second Coming.

Hosea 6:2 reads, **"<u>After two days</u> He will revive us; <u>On the third day</u> He will raise us** (Israel) **up, That we may live in His sight."** After 2 days or 2000 years the Lord will raise up Israel and restore them that they may live with Him. As Rom. 11:25b reads, after **"the fullness of the Gentiles has come in."**

Lazarus' Resurrection—

John 11:6 reads, **"So when He (Jesus) heard that he (Lazarus) was sick, He stayed two more days in the place He was."** The hidden message is that Jesus will raise up the Jews (Zech. 12:10) after 2 days or 2000 years.

3. <u>This Age = 6 days or 6000 years???</u>

<u>Mount of Transfiguration</u>—

Matt. 17:1 reads, **"Now after six days Jesus took Peter, James, and John his brother, brought them up on a high mountain by themselves."**

Mark 9:2 reads, **"Now after six days Jesus took Peter, James, and John, and led them up on a high mountain apart by themselves; and He was transfigured before them."** After 6000 years Jesus will make Himself seen by the entire resurrected Christian body.

Luke 9:28 reads, **"And it came to pass about eight days after these sayings, that He took Peter, John, and James and went up on the mountain to pray."**

In the previous verse of Luke it reads, **"But I (Jesus) tell you truly, there are some standing here (meaning Peter, John, and James) who shall not taste death till they see the kingdom of God."** (Luke 9:27) A similar saying can be found in the preceding verse of the other two Gospels.

4. <u>Marriage and Wedding Banquets</u>

Jacob's Marriages

Jacob asked Laban if he could marry his daughter, Rachel. Laban agreed if Jacob would work for him for seven years. Jacob agreed to work for Laban seven years. After seven years Jacob and Rachel were to consummate their marriage. Laban tricked Jacob by giving him Leah, Rachel's older sister, instead of Rachel. In the morning when Jacob found out he was livid. Laban told Jacob that in his country the older daughter must marry first, and if Jacob would agree to work for him another seven years he would give him Rachel for his wife once Jacob had fulfilled his seven-day honeymoon with Leah. Jacob agreed. So Jacob married two sisters in a weeks time. The marriages of Jacob is recorded in Genesis 29.

Jacob's marriage is a type of Christ's marriage to the Church (Jacob's marriage to Leah) and to the nation Israel (Jacob's marriage to Rachel, the one he loved the most). I believe Christ will consummate the marriage to the Church seven years before he consummates the marriage to the nation Israel.

Jesus' <u>parable of the Faithful Servant</u> and the Evil Servant

Luke 12:35-40 reads, **"Let your waist be girded and your lamps burning; and you yourselves be like men who wait for their master, when he will return from the wedding, that when he comes and knocks they may open to him immediately. Blessed are those servants whom the master, when he comes, will find watching. Assuredly, I say to you that he will gird himself and have them sit down to eat, and will come and serve them. And if he should come in the second watch, or come in the third watch, and find them so, blessed are those servants. But know this, that if the master of the house had known what hour the thief would come, he would have watched and not allowed his house to be broken into. Therefore you also be ready, for the Son of Man is coming at an hour you do not expect."**

In verse 35, the servants are warned to be ready to eat (having your waist be girded) and with faith (your lamps burning). In verse 36 the servants are to watch and wait for their Lord for <u>when He returns from the wedding</u>, He will knock and they should open the door immediately. In verse 37, the Lord will gird Himself (preparing to eat) and have the servants sit down to eat and <u>the Lord will serve them</u>.

In these verses our Lord has been to a wedding. I believe the wedding is our wedding—Christ and the Church.

And I believe we will have the wedding ceremony when we are raptured. In the rapture, the <u>saved</u> people will be <u>taken</u> and the unsaved will be left as stated in the parable about ten virgins.

The fact that not all of the people were taken in the rapture would support the doctrine of millennialism.

5. <u>Jewish Festivals</u>

The Jews were commanded by God to celebrate seven feasts every year. These seven feasts are held at three different times throughout the year—early spring, late spring, and early fall. (See Lev. 23)

Early spring—	1)	Passover	14th day of the first month (Nisan)
	2)	<u>Feast of Unleavened Bread</u>	15th thru the 21st day of the first month
	3)	Feast of Firstfruits	day after first Sabbath during Passover
Late spring—	4)	<u>Feast of Weeks</u> or Pentecost	49th day after Feast of Firstfruits
Late summer—	5)	Feast of Trumpets	first day of the seventh month (Tishri)
	6)	Day of Atonement	tenth day of the seventh month
	7)	Feast of Tabernacles	15th thru 22nd day of the seventh month

Jesus validated the first four feasts (Col. 2:16-17) during His First Coming by His dying and rising, and by sending the Holy Spirit to establish His Church on earth.

Will He validate the last three feasts during His Second Coming?

I believe He will. If He does validate these three feasts it will take at least 22 days to accomplish this, and it will not be over in one big flash.

The Feast of Firstfruits (Lev. 23:14), the Feast of Weeks (Lev. 23:21), the Day of Atonement (Lev. 23:31), and the Feast of Tabernacles (Lev. 23:41) are to be observed forever.

CHAPTER 10

DEFINITION OF TERMS DEALING WITH END TIME EVENTS

Apocalyptic literature is a type of literature which uncovers or reveals something that beforehand was hidden. For example, Daniel 12:4 reads, 'shut up the words and seal the book until the time of the end'. Revelation is the book that reveals much of Daniel.

Eschatology is the study of end time events.

Inaugurated eschatology embraces everything that Scriptures teach concerning the believer's present possession and enjoyment of blessings.

Future eschatology focuses on events which still lie in the future, such as the resurrection, judgment, and new heavens and new earth.

Hermeneutics are the principles used for the interpretation of Scripture.

Millennialism is the doctrine that Christ will reign on earth for a period of 1000 years.

Premillennialism is the doctrine that the second coming of Christ precedes the millennial reign of Christ.

Dispensation, as referred to in theology, is the distribution or dispensing of good and evil by God to man (Webster's Collegiate Dictionary). See Jeremiah 42:6 & 10 in KJV for the evil God sends to man.

Dispensational premillennialism is the doctrine that the saved people, i.e., those living and dead saints, will go up to meet the Lord in the air at the rapture, and the unsaved will stay on earth to go through the Great Tribulation. After a period of time, the Lord will make His Second Coming appearance to earth to reign for 1000 years. During His 1000 year reign, there will be some more people who will be saved. After 1000 years the unsaved will face the White Throne Judgment.

Historic, as referred to in historic premillennialism, is the doctrine that only the saved people will be resurrected at the rapture. Then, the saints will make an immediate return to earth with Christ to reign with Him for 1000 years. The unsaved will be resurrected after the 1000 years to face the White Throne Judgment.

Postmillennialism is the doctrine that the second coming of Christ follows the millennium. [Postmillennialists believe people will beat their swords into plowshares, the leopard will lie down with the young goat, and a child shall die when he is 100 years old during the church age. As sin during the church age has gotten worse and worse, postmillennialism has dropped out of favor.]

Amillennialism is the doctrine that Christ will not reign on earth for a period of 1000 years.

[This doctrine requires much of Scripture in Isaiah, Ezekiel, Daniel, Hosea, Joel, Amos, Micah, Nahum, Zephaniah, Zechariah, and Revelation to be interpreted symbolically and not to be taken literally.]

Rapture is the catching up of the Christians to meet the Lord in the air. The premillennialists believe the rapture will occur relative to another event called the tribulation period. The tribulation period is taken to be approximately 7 years long. There are people who believe the rapture will occur before the tribulation, called pre-tribulationists; during the 7-year period, called mid-tribulationists; or after the tribulation, called post-tribulationists.

Tribulation period, as referred to by premillennialists and end time event proponents, is 2520 days in length. The tribulation period starts when the nation of Israel signs an agreement with the Antichrist.

Great tribulation period, as referred to by premillennialists and end time event proponents, is the last 1260 days of the tribulation period.

The Dragon is Satan spoken of by John in Revelation 12:3. The Antichrist is the 'beast from the sea' in Revelation 13:1. The False Prophet is the 'beast from the land' in Revelation 13:11.

CHAPTER 11
THOUGHT PROVOKING QUESTIONS ABOUT THE BIBLE

1. Why, after each day of creation, God saw that it was good except the second day? After the second day the Bible just says 'it was so'.

   First Day: God created light. It was good.
   Second Day: God created heaven. It was so.
   Third Day: God created earth and vegetation. It was good.
   Fourth Day: God created sun, moon, and stars. It was good.
   Fifth Day: God created fish and fowl. It was good.
   Sixth Day: God created animals and man. It was good.

I believe the angels were already created. Lucifer and one-third of the angels had already rebelled against God. And God created heaven and He set aside heaven as the abode for the rebellious angels. That is why God did not say, "It was good" on the second day.

2. According to the Bible, what two things were not created during the six day creation?

Darkness and waters. And possibly the angels. Darkness (and waters) were created before the six day creation. Is. 45:7.

3. Has Satan and his angels been cast out of heaven yet (10/12/2002)?

No, I don't believe that he has. We know that Satan still had access to heaven in Job's day as told in Job 1:6-12.

Was Satan cast out of heaven at the time of Jesus' death and resurrection?

No, I don't believe he was. The Bible states in Eph. 6:12, **"For we do not wrestle against flesh and blood, but against principalities, against powers, against the rulers of the darkness of this age, against spiritual hosts of wickedness in the heavenly places."** I believe Satan still has access to heaven, and he will be thrown out of heaven during the <u>Great Tribulation</u> as foretold in Rev. 12:7-17.

I believe that Satan will have access to heaven until <u>Matthew 24:29</u> and Mark 13:24 where it says, **"powers of the heavens will be shaken."** However, this could be referring to the powers of the physical heavens, such as, gravitational forces. Or both interpretations could be fulfilled.

4. What is heaven like?

Before paradise was lost the world was perfect. There was an abundance of plants and animals that grew and reproduced after their kind. I don't think that there was any death or dying at that time. If heaven is paradise regained then we should expect it to be like it was before the fall of man into sin with one exception. Man will be like the angels. They will be neither male nor female (Gal. 3:28). And they do not marry nor are given in marriage (Matt. 22:30).

If there are animals in heaven will there be any dogs? Rev. 22:15. Or snakes? Gen. 3:15. Or will animals reproduce? Maybe they are sexless too. Or will they defecate or perspire? Will man defecate or perspire? Will there be a total elimination of the Second Law of Thermodynamics, i.e., the clock never runs down or gets rusty?

I believe that if there will be animals in heaven, and that they too will be non reproductive. Man will be a vegetarian. He doesn't need to eat anything, but if he does it will be wholly consumed with no waste material or energy. He will not defecate or perspire or get tired or need rest or sleep. If man has an accident and injures himself he will be healed by the leaves of the tree of life. Rev. 22:2.

5. Is God the only one who is Omniscient, Omnipotent, and Omnipresent?

I think that He is. I don't believe the angels have that capability. God is the only one who is all—knowing, all-powerful, and all-present. Satan does not know what I am thinking, so if I don't verbalize my feelings and show my emotions, he has no way of knowing my feelings about certain things or about certain people.

6. How was Arphaxad the father of Salah (Shelah) who was the father of Eber and also Cainan who was the father of Shelah? Compare Genesis 11:24 with Luke 3:35-36.

Genesis Genealogy: Arphaxad—Salah—Eber
Luke Genealogy: Arphaxad—Cainan—Shelah—Eber

Possible solution: Cainan died before his wife could bear him any children. Cainan's brother, Salah, married Cainan's wife and had a child called Eber and raised up Eber for Cainan. Matthew 22:24.

Argument against this solution: Eber was not of Cainan's seed which is what Luke 3 would lead one to believe.

7. What is Luke's genealogy? It differs with Matthew's genealogy.

Matthew's genealogy is the royal line of David from Solomon to Joseph the stepfather of Jesus. [Matthew's genealogy leaves out several generations. (See II Kings.)]

Luke's genealogy is the line from David's son, Nathan, to Mary the mother of Jesus. But the genealogy never mentions Mary by name.

8. Was Nathan David's son or David's stepson, i.e., Bathsheba's son by Uriah?

I believe that Nathan was David's son. If he was David's stepson Mary, mother of Jesus, couldn't be of David's seed. Uriah was a Hittite. Ex. 33:2.

9. Did the Holy Spirit implant a fertilized egg into the Virgin Mary's womb, in other words, did God use Mary as a surrogate mother, or did the Holy Spirit fertilize one of the Virgin Mary's eggs?

I believe the Holy Spirit fertilized one of the Virgin Mary's eggs, and as a result, Jesus the Christ was born. Jesus is the <u>Seed of David</u>. The Lord said to David, **"When your days are fulfilled and you rest with your fathers, I will set up your seed after you, who will come from your body, and I will establish his kingdom."** (2 Sam. 7:12; NKJV). If the Holy Spirit supplied a fertilized egg to Mary's womb then Jesus couldn't be an ancestor of David. That is why Jesus is called the <u>Son of Man</u> or true Man, as well as the Son of God or true God.

10. How does (did) sin propagate throughout generations of mankind?

Gen. 2:7 says that God breathed into Adam's nostrils the breath of life and man became a living being. This is something that God did not do with any other creature. So, man became a human being, which has God's immortality and the ability to pass this immortality on to his offspring through his sperm.

God caused Adam to fall into a deep sleep. While Adam slept God took one of Adam's ribs and made Eve. God made Eve from Adam. The Bible doesn't tell us whether God breathed into Eve the breath of life like He did with Adam. I personally don't believe He did. Anyway, Eve's life and immortality most likely was passed from Adam. Adam was perfect and now Eve was perfect. The two became husband and wife (Gen. 2:21-24).

Eve succumbed to eating the forbidden fruit first. Before any of Eve's eggs were fertilized she ate of the tree of knowledge of good and evil. Then Adam did also eat of the forbidden fruit.

I believe that through Adam's sperm (seed) only, life and immortality passes on to each succeeding generation. I don't believe that original sin is propagated on to Eve's offspring through her eggs. (I may have to rethink this if human sperm can be produced in the laboratory; i.e., without male participation.)

When the Holy Spirit entered the Virgin Mary He must have purged all sin from Mary's egg. Otherwise, I would have to believe that the Virgin Mary was a surrogate mother since Mary's egg would have been sinful.

That is why the Bible always refers to Adam as the chief culprit and not Eve. 1 Cor. 15:22 reads, **"For as in Adam all die, even so in Christ's all shall be made alive."** And Romans 5:12 reads, **"Therefore, just as <u>through one man</u> sin entered the world, and death through sin, and thus death spread to all men, because all sinned."** Since Adam sinned all his descendants are sinners. Adam's living sperm passed this curse on to each succeeding generation.

Note: We often think of physical death as the extinction of life, but in reality, we should think of death as either eternal separation from God or, for a Christian, eternal residence with God.

11. Should we baptize infants? Or wait until they are old enough to make up their own mind?

Arguments for infant baptism: **"Go ye therefore, and teach all nations, baptizing them in the name of the Father, and of the Son, and of the Holy Ghost."** Matthew 28:19. Infants can not reason. Some imbeciles never can reason. Some infants die before they can reason. It is God that gives man the Holy Spirit to believe anyway. Besides, man baptizes with water, but it is Jesus who baptizes us (man) with the Holy Spirit. See Matthew 3:11. Judas undoubtedly was baptized with water, and he is in hell. See John 17:12. The malefactor on the cross was probably not baptized with water but was baptized by Jesus with the Holy Spirit, and he went to be with Jesus that very day. See Luke 23:43. Does believing come first or baptism with water come first? Neither. Baptism with the Holy Spirit comes first; whether an infant or an adult. In fact, the infant could be a fetus, like John the Baptist was. See Luke 1:41.

Argument against infant baptism: We should believe and be baptized. And the little children and the mentally challenged can not believe so they should not be baptized until they are older.

12. Are the unbelievers (the unsaved) going to spend eternity in the Lake of Fire?

Argument for: The rich man wants Lazarus to warn his people. Luke 16:20-31.

Anyone not found written in the Book of Life will be cast into the Lake of Fire, as will Death and Hades (Hell). This is the Second Death. Rev. 20:13-15.

13. Was Ishmael a believer or an unbeliever?

I think the Bible tells us that he was a believer. Genesis 25:17 tells us that Ishmael was 137 years old when he gave up the ghost and died, and was gathered unto his people. I believe the phrase **"gathered to his people"** has a specific meaning in the Bible. See Gen. 25:8 for Abraham; Gen. 25:17 for Ishmael; Gen. 35:29 for Isaac; Gen. 49:29 and 49:33 for Jacob; Num. 20:24, 20:26 and 27:13 for Aaron; Num. 31:2 and Deut. 32:50 for Moses; Judges 2:10 for Joshua and that generation that conquered Canaan. Esau did not make the list.

Also, being gathered unto his people would mean that Ishmael was with Abraham, his father. And, referring to the rich man and Lazarus in Luke 16:19-31, Lazarus was in the bosom of Abraham whereas the rich man was not, and there was a great gulf between the rich man and Abraham.

The Lord said to Moses, **"And when you have seen it (Canaan), you also shall be gathered to your people, as Aaron your brother was gathered."** Gen. 27:13.

For someone who is not saved see what the Lord says about Pharaoh king of Egypt in Ezekiel 29:5. **"You (Pharaoh) shall not be picked up or gathered."**

"Do not gather my soul together with sinners." Psalm 26:9.

"They shall not be gathered nor buried; they shall be like refuse on the face of the earth." Jer. 8:2b.

"They shall not be lamented, or gathered, or buried; they shall become refuse on the ground." Jer. 25:33.

"Now we beseech you, brethren, by the coming of our Lord Jesus Christ, and by our gathering together unto him." 2 Thess. 2:1.

14. Whose wedding did the Master attend in the parable "The Faithful Servant and the Evil Servant" in Luke 12:35-37?

It reads, **"Let your waist be girded and your lamps burning; and you yourselves be like men who wait for their master, <u>when he will return from the wedding</u>, that when he comes and knocks they may open to him immediately. Blessed are those servants whom the master, when he comes, will find watching. Assuredly, I say to you that he will gird himself and have them sit down to eat, and <u>will come and serve them</u>."** (NKJV).

The question is whose wedding did the Master return from? I believe it is our wedding. Jesus and His Church.

And He **will come and serve them**. Who is them? My interpretation is that they, the servants, are the people who became believers on earth after the rapture.

15. Where in Old Testament is there an analogy of the <u>pretribulation rapture</u> and those left behind to go through the tribulation?

Jacob married Leah seven days before he married Rachel. Leah is a type of Christian Church where we become Christ's Bride seven years before Rachel, a type of Jewish believers, that become Christ's Second Bride. Genesis 29:15-30.

16. Has Ezekiel 29:8-16 been ultimately fulfilled?

I don't believe it has. The land of Egypt has not been made desolate and waste, where neither foot of man shall pass through it nor foot of beast pass through it, and made uninhabited for forty years, and at the end of forty years God will bring them back to Egypt.

If Egypt has never been made desolate and waste for forty years yet, the <u>amillennialists</u> are in error when they say that Jesus Christ's Second Coming to earth is imminent. The amillennialists would have to believe that forty years remains yet before the end of the world could occur. Therefore, Christ's Second Coming could not be imminent as they say it is. Lutherans, like Catholics, are amillennialists. Martin Luther did not go far enough with the reformation. He probably had bigger fish to fry.

17a. Will the believer get a new body when he dies?

Yes. A person's physical body, including the heart and brain, will return to dust from which it came (Eccl. 12:7), and when believers are resurrected we will get a new body. The dead believers will be resurrected with an incorruptible body (1 Cor. 15:50-58). The living believers at the rapture will be changed to an incorruptible body in the twinkling of an eye.

17b. Will the nonbeliever also get a new body?

I don't know but I don't think so.

18a. Will the believer's soul die? [The soul is what makes you you. A person's personality.]

No, it does not. Jesus did not leave His soul in hell, neither wilt thou suffer thine Holy One to see corruption (Acts 2:27). A believer's soul never dies as implied in John 11:25-26 and stated as a fact in James 5:20.

18b. Will the unbeliever's soul die?

Yes. A nonbeliever's soul is dead already (from conception). But, the soul of a nonbeliever will die a <u>second death</u> (Rev. 20:14-15).

19a. Will the believer's spirit die?

No. It never dies. The believer's spirit returns to God who gave it (Eccl. 12:7), so a believer's spirit never dies.

19b. What about the nonbeliever's spirit? Will the unbeliever's spirit die?

No. Jesus said, "Depart from Me, you cursed, into the everlasting fire prepared for the devil and his angels," in Matt. 25:41, "and these will go away into everlasting punishment," in verse 46. The unbeliever will 'suffer the vengance of eternal fire' (Jude 7).

20.   What does it mean to be "born again" as used in John 3:3?

Born once die twice. The unbeliever has a physical birth only. He will have a physical death and a <u>spiritual death</u>.

Born twice die once. The believer has a physical birth and a Spiritual rebirth. He will have only a physical death.

The believers will be raised in the "first resurrection". The "second resurrection" will only consists of those people who experience the "second death". Rev. 20.

CHAPTER 12

RECOVERING THE REMNANT OF ISRAEL FOR THE SECOND TIME

Remnant of Israel brought back for the Second Time.

It shall come to pass in that day that the Lord shall set His hand again the second time to recover the remnant of His people who are left, from Assyria and Egypt, from Pathros and Cush, from Elam and <u>Shinar</u>, from Hamath and the islands of the sea. Isaiah 11:11. (The passages quoted here are from NKJV.)

<u>Questions:</u>
What does this mean?

Who is 'the remnant'? And who are 'His people'?

Isaiah calls them His people. I am His (God's) people, but so is Israel His people, or at the very least, the believing Jews. Isaiah was writing to the Jews of his day. I believe that Israel is the remnant of His people, and they are from the four corners of the earth (Is. 11:12). They are a remnant from all over the earth, not just from a certain geographical area.

What is meant by 'that day'?

Isaiah starts out in verse 11, **"It shall come to pass in that day . . .".** This is prophecy. **"It shall come to pass . . ."** means it will happen in the future.

That day, or the day of trouble, or the day of revenge, or such references are another way of saying the end of this age in the Bible. There are over 135 references to 'day' in the Bible when referring to the <u>end times</u>. If you want to know where the references to the end time are in the Bible I have nearly 300 references listed. See <u><References to 'The Day'></u> for the many passages discussing day.

In fact, Isaiah is prophesying in all of <u>Chapter 11</u>. In the first two verses Isaiah is prophesying Jesus' First Coming. This has happened. The rest of Chapter 11 is about the end of this age. This is yet to happen. You can find this out by reading the second part of verse 4. **(Jesus) shall strike the earth with the rod of His mouth, and with the breath of His lips He shall slay the wicked.** And if you are still not convinced this is yet to happen then read verses 6 through 9. Hmm, this sounds like it could be when Christ rules on earth.

What is the significance of **'the second time'** in Isaiah 11:11? When was the first time?

Isaiah was written between 740 and 700 B.C. The ten Northern Tribes were known as Israel. They were taken captive by Assyria in 723 to 721 B.C. The two Southern Tribes were known as Judah. Judah, and in particular, Jerusalem was spared from being captured by Assyria by God as a result of Isaiah and Hezekiah's prayers. We have no scriptural references that the Northern Tribes returned to Israel. Maybe this was because the Assyrians never removed all of the Israelites from Israel. (The Assyrians that settled in Israel at that time became known as the Samaritans.) The question is when was the first time if this is not the first time? I will answer that.

First Jewish Diaspora

Nebuchadnezzar captured the land of Israel in 586 B.C., and he carried all of Israel off to Babylon.

Cyrus, King of Persia, signed the release of Israel in c. 536 B.C. giving the Jews the right to go home.

Second Jewish Diaspora

Hadrian, Emperor of Rome, ordered all the Jews out of the land of Israel or be killed in A.D. 135. (Hadrian also changed the name of Jerusalem to Capitolina.)

The United Nations voted to make Israel a nation in a day, May 14, 1948. This was another fulfillment of Isaiah's prophecy in verse 8 of chapter 66. **Who has heard such a thing? Who has seen such things? Shall the earth be made to give birth in one day? Or shall a nation be born at once?** Isaiah 66:8.

In summary, Israel is back in the land a second time and will never be pulled up from the land again.

"Behold, the days are coming," says the Lord, **"When the plowman shall overtake the reaper, and the treader of grapes him who sows seed; the mountains shall drip with sweet wine, and all the hills shall flow with it. I will bring back the captives of My people Israel; they shall build the waste cities and inhabit them; they shall plant vineyards and drink wine from them; they shall also make gardens and eat fruit from them. I will plant them in their land, and no longer shall they be pulled up from the land I have given them,"** says the Lord your God. Amos 9:13-15. This prophecy is being fulfilled today. I believe that we are in the end times.

So, if you are one who believes that God is through with the Nation of Israel, which is what I was taught in confirmation instruction, that teaching is wrong.

CHAPTER 13

REFERENCES TO 'THE DAY'

I did a search in the New King James Version (NKJV) of the Bible looking for passages which have the word 'day' in it that possibly deals with the end time. There were several hundred verses in the Bible that use 'day' as a noun for describing the end time.

1. The Day of The Lord of Hosts—Isaiah 2:12
2. The Day of Punishment—Isaiah 10:3
3. The Day of The Lord—Isaiah 13:6; Ezekiel 13:5; Ezekiel 30:3; Joel 1:15; Joel 2:1; Joel 2:11; Joel 3:14; Amos 5:18; Amos 5:20; Zephaniah 1:7; Zephaniah 1:14; Zechariah 14:1; I Thessalonians 5:2; II Peter 3:10
4. The Day of His Fierce Anger—Isaiah 13:13; Lamentations 1:12
5. The Day The Lord Gives You Rest—Isaiah 14:3
6. The Day of Grief and Desperate Sorrow—Isaiah 17:11
7. A Day of Trouble—Isaiah 22:5; Ezekiel 7:7
8. The Day of The East Wind—Isaiah 27:8
9. The Day of The Great Slaughter—Isaiah 30:25
10. The Day That The Lord Binds Up The Bruises of His People—Isaiah 30:26
11. The Day of The Lord's Vengence—Isaiah 34:8
12. A Day of Trouble and Rebuke and Blasphemy—Isaiah 37:3; II Kings 19:3
13. The Day of Salvation—Isaiah 49:8
14. The Day of Vengeance of Our God—Isaiah 61:2
15. The Day of Vengeance—Isaiah 63:4; Proverbs 6:34
16. The Day of Slaughter—Jeremiah 12:3
17. The Day of Affliction—Jeremiah 16:19
18. The Day of Doom—Jeremiah 17:17; Jeremiah 17:18; Jeremiah 51:2; Amos 6:3; Job 21:30
19. The Day of Their Calamity—Jeremiah 18:17; Jeremiah 46:21; Deuteronomy 32:35
20. The Time of Jacob's Trouble—Jeremiah 30:7
21. The Day of The Lord God of Hosts—Jeremiah 46:10
22. A Day of Vengeance—Jeremiah 46:10
23. The Day That You Have Announced—Lamentations 1:21
24. The Day of His Anger—Lamentations 2:1
25. The Day We Have Waited For—Lamentations 2:16
26. The Day of Your Anger—Lamentations 2:21
27. The Day of The Lord's Anger—Lamentations 2:22; Zephaniah 2:2; Zephaniah 2:3
28. Behold, The Day—Ezekiel 7:10
29. The Day of The Wrath of The Lord—Ezekiel 7:19
30. The Day of Indignation—Ezekiel 22:24
31. The Day of Your Fall—Ezekiel 26:18; Ezekiel 32:10

32. The Day—Ezekiel 30:2; Ezekiel 30.3; Joel 1:15; Zephaniah 3:8; Malachi 4:1; I Corinthians 3:13
33. A Day of Clouds—Ezekiel 30:3
34. The Day of Egypt—Ezekiel 30:9
35. The Day That I Am Glorified—Ezekiel 39:13
36. The Day of Jezreel—Hosea 1:11
37. The Day of Rebuke—Hosea 5:9
38. The Day of Our King—Hosea 7:5
39. The Appointed Day—Hosea 9:5
40. The Day of The Feast of The Lord—Hosea 9:5
41. The Days of Punishment—Hosea 9:7
42. The Days of Recompense—Hosea 9:7
43. The Day of Darkness and Gloominess—Joel 2:2; Zephaniah 1:15
44. A Day of Clouds and Thick Darkness—Joel 2:2; Zephaniah 1:15
45. The Great and Terrible Day of The Lord—Joel 2:31
46. The Day of Battle—Amos 1:14; Zechariah 14:3; Psalms 140:7; Proverbs 21:31
47. The Day of The Whirlwind—Amos 1:14
48. The Day of The Lord Upon All The Nations—Obadiah 15
49. The Day of Your Watchman and Your Punishment—Micah 7:4
50. The Day of Trouble—Nahum 1:7; Habakkuk 3:16; Psalms 20:1; Psalms 50:15
51. The Day of His Preparation—Nahum 2:3
52. The Day of The Lord's Sacrifice—Zephaniah 1:8
53. The Great Day of The Lord—Zephaniah 1:14
54. A Day of Wrath—Zephaniah 1:15
55. A Day of Trouble and Distress—Zephaniah 1:15
56. A Day of Devastation and Desolation—Zephaniah 1:15
57. A Day of Trumpet and Alarm—Zephaniah 1:16
58. The Day of The Lord's Wrath—Zephaniah 1:18
59. The Day of His Coming—Malachi 3:2
60. The Great and Dreadful Day of The Lord—Malachi 4:5
61. The Day of My Calamity—II Samuel 22:19
62. The Day of His Wrath—Job 20:28; Psalms 110:5
63. The Day of Wrath—Job 21:30; Proverbs 11:4
64. The Day of Battle and War—Job 38:23
65. The Day of My Trouble—Psalms 59:16; Psalms 77:2; Psalms 86:7; Psalms 102:2
66. The Day of Your Power—Psalms 110:3
67. The Day of Adversity—Proverbs 24:10
68. The Day When The Keepers of The House Tremble—Ecclesiastes 12:3
69. The Day of His Espousals—Song of Solomon 3:11
70. The Day of The Gladness of His Heart—Song of Solomon 3:11
71. The Day of Judgment—Matthew 10:15; Matthew 11:24; Matthew 12:36; Mark 6:11; II Peter 2:9; I John 4:17
72. The Son of Man Will Be In His Day—Luke 17:24
73. The Day When The Son of Man Is Revealed—Luke 17:30
74. The Great and Notable Day of The Lord—Acts 2:20

75. A Day On Which He Will Judge The World In Righteousness By The Man Whom He Has Ordained—Acts 17:31
76. The Day of Wrath and Revelation of The Righteous Judgment of God—Romans 2:5
77. The Day of Our Lord Jesus Christ—I Corinthians 1:8
78. The Day of The Lord Jesus—II Corinthians 1:14
79. The Day of Redemption—Ephesians 4:30
80. The Day of Jesus Christ—<u>Philippians</u> 1:6
81. The Day of Christ—Philippians 1:10; Philippians 2:16
82. The Day of Judgment and Perdition of Ungodly Men—II Peter 3:7
83. The Day of God—II Peter 3:12
84. The Judgment of The Great Day—Jude 6
85. The Great Day of His Wrath—Revelation 6:17
86. That Day There Shall Be a Root of Jesse—Isaiah 11:10
87. That Day That The Lord Shall Set His Hand Again The Second Time—Isaiah 11:11
88. That Great Day of God Almighty—Revelation 16:14
(138 Total)

OTHER REFERENCES TO THE END TIME:

<u>Indignation</u>—Deuteronomy 29:28; Job 10:17; Psalms 69:24; 78:49; 102:10; Isaiah 10:5 & 25; 13:5; 26:20; 30:27 & 30; 34:2; 66:14; Jeremiah 10:10; 15:17; 50:25; Lamentations 2:6; Ezekiel 21:31; 22:24 & 31; Daniel 8:19; Micah 7:9; Nahum 1:6; <u>Habakkuk</u> 3:12; Zephaniah 3:8; Malachi 1:4; Romans 2:8; Hebrews 10:27; Revelation 14:10
(29 Total)

<u>Trouble</u>—II Kings 19:3; I Chronicles 22:14; II Chronicles 15:4; 29:8; 32:18; Nehemiah 9:27 & 32; Job 3:26; 38:23; Psalms 9:9 & 13; 10:1; 13:4; 20:1; 22:11; 25:17 & 22; 27:5; 31:7 & 9; 34:6 & 17; 37:39; 41:1; 46:1; 50:15; 54:7; 59:16; 60:11; 66:14; 69:17; 71:20; 73:5; 77:2; 78:49; 81:7; 86:7; 88:3; 91:15; 102:2; 104:29; 107:6, 19, 26 & 28, 108:12; 116:3; 119:143; 138:7; 142:2; 143:11; Proverbs 11:8; 12:13; 25:19; Isaiah 8:22; 22:5; 26:16; 30:6; 32:10 & 11; 33:2; 37:3; 46:7; 57:20; 65:16 & 23; Jeremiah 2:27 & 28; 8:15; 11:12 & 14; 14:8 & 19; 30:7; Lamentations 1:21; Ezekiel 7:7; 26:18; 27:35; Daniel 12:1; Nahum 1:7; Habakkuk 3:16; Zephaniah 1:15
(82 Total)

<u>Whirlwind</u>—II Kings 2:1 & 11; Job 37:9; 38:1; 40:6; Psalms 58:9; Proverbs 1:27; 10:25; Isaiah 5:28; 17:13; 21:1; 40:24; 41:16; 66:15; Jeremiah 4:13; 23:19; 25:32; 30:23; Ezekiel 1:4; Daniel 11:40; <u>Hosea</u> 8:7; Amos 1:14; Nahum 1:3; Habakkuk 3:14; Zechariah 7:14; 9:14.
(26 Total)

<u>Woman In Labor</u>—Genesis 3:16; 35:16 & 17; II Kings 19:3; Psalms 48:6; Isaiah 13:8; 21:3; 23:4; 26:17; 37:3; 42:14; 54:1; 66:7-9; Jeremiah 4:31; 6:24; 13:21; 22:23; 30:6; 31:8; 48:41; 49:22 & 24; 50:43; Hosea 13:13; Micah 4:9 & 10; 5:3; Matthew 24:8; Mark 13:8; John 16:21; I Thessalonians 5:3; Revelation 12:2.
(34 Total)

CHAPTER 14

ISRAEL'S THIRD TEMPLE

Israel has had two temples in the past. Will they have a <u>third temple</u> sometime in the future?

Israel's First Temple was initially started under King Solomon, son of King David, in 969 B.C. The First Temple existed for 383 years. It was destroyed by <u>King Nebuchadnezzar</u> of the Babylonian Empire in 586 B.C. Nebuchadnezzar took most of the remaining Jews and exiled them to Babylon along with the Jews King Jehoiachin. The Jews were in exile for 70 years. The 70 years were prophesied in Jer. 25:11-12. During this 70-year period the Medo-Persians defeated the Babylonian Empire. <u>King Cyrus</u> of the Medo-Persian Empire freed the Jews and allowed them to return to their own land in c.536 B.C. Cyrus freeing the Jews was also prophesied in Isaiah 44:24 to 45:2.

The Second Temple was begun under Governor Zerubbabel of Judah in 520 B.C. and was dedicated in 516 B.C. This is the temple that existed when Jesus was born and all the while God was with us. It was sometimes referred to as King Herod's Temple because he remodeled it and made it so much more elaborate than when first constructed under Zerubbabel. This temple was destroyed by General Titus of the Roman Empire in A.D. 70 when the Jews rebelled. The destruction of this temple was also prophesied by Matthew 24:2.

Will there be a <u>Third Temple</u>? Yes, and again I say yes. And maybe even a fourth temple.

When will it be constructed? I don't know. But for sure, there will be a temple during the <u>great tribulation</u> and Christ's millennial reign.

How do I know? The Bible tells me so. In Paul's second letter to the Thessalonians the Bible says that there will be a temple in which the son of perdition will exalt himself during the tribulation. In chapters 40 through 44 of Ezekiel it tells us of the architectural floor plan of the temple existing during <u>millennial age</u>.

Is it possible that a temple could be built today? Yes, it is possible but I don't think so. If the Jews were to start to build a temple today it wouldn't be God's Holy Place of worship since the non Messianic, i.e., non Christian, Jews do not believe in the Triune God; Father, Son, and Holy Spirit.

If the 'Third Temple', the 'Tribulation Temple', and the 'Millennial Temple' are one and the same, it will probably be constructed after the Church is raptured out of the world and before the great tribulation begins. I believe that there will be repentant Jews who will finally come to their senses after the Christians are taken out of the world. The Jews will sign a peace agreement talked about in Daniel 9 and the temple will be constructed. **"Then he** (the

Antichrist) **shall confirm a covenant with many for one week"**, or for approximately a seven-year period. (NKJV; Dan. 9:27a). [For the definition of 'week' see Chapter 7, Dating Christ's Death and Resurrection.]

The Bible suggests to us in Matthew 24:15 & 21 that a temple exists before the great tribulation period. **"Therefore when you see the 'abomination of desolation,' spoken of by Daniel the prophet, standing in the holy place"** (verse 15). **"For then there will be great tribulation, such as has not been since the beginning of the world until this time, no, nor ever shall be."** (verse 21). In II Thessalonians chapter 2 the Bible tells us of a temple during the great tribulation period. **"Let no one deceive you by any means; for that Day will not come unless the falling away comes first, and the man of sin (the Antichrist) is revealed, the son of perdition, who opposes and exalts himself above all that is called God or that is worshiped, so that he sits as God in the temple of God, showing himself that he is God."** (II Thess. 2:3-4).

Jesus Christ will return to earth at the end of the great tribulation and slay all those people who do not believe in Him (Rev. 19:11-21). Jesus Christ will have all the saints in heaven with Him (I Thess. 3:13 and Rev. 19:11). [This is Christ's Second Coming. He does not touch down when He comes for the Church.] Jesus will capture the Antichrist and the False Prophet and will throw them alive into the Lake of Fire. Christ will also bind up Satan with chains and throw him into hell for one thousand years.

If the tribulation temple is the millennial temple I believe that this temple will be cleansed at this point. The cleansing of the tribulation temple will be necessary to make it the house of God talked about in Ezekiel 40 through 44 and Zechariah 14:16-21.

How will this cleansing of the temple come about? I don't know, but here is something to think about. Could the cleansing of the temple have something to do with the original seven (Lev. 23), or now eight, Jewish Festivals? The Feasts of Lights, or Hanukkah, is the eighth feast. It was instituted when the Israelites under the Maccabeans took back and cleansed the temple in 164 B.C.

In Daniel, the Bible tells us that God's people will be blessed after the abomination of desolation is set up. Could this be the cleansing of the temple after the Antichrist profanes the temple by sitting in the temple and calling himself God? **"And from the time that the daily sacrifice is taken away, and the abomination of desolation is set up, there shall be one thousand two hundred and ninety days. Blessed is he who waits, and comes to one thousand three hundred and thirty-five days."** (Dan. 12:11-12.) The length of time between the first day of the Feast of Tabernacles and the Feast of Lights (Hanukkah) is 75 days = 1335 days—1260 days. The beginning of the great tribulation is the start of this period, i.e., when the daily sacrifices are taken away. So, maybe there will be a Christ associated historical event with the last four Jewish Festivals (Rosh Hashanah, Yom Kippur, Tabernacles, Hanukkah) as there were with the first four Jewish Festivals (Passover, Unleavened Bread, First Fruits, Pentecost).

If the tribulation temple is destroyed in the great tribulation or if the temple is not built to the correct architectural specifications then it can't be the millennial temple as I proposed above. Then I believe the millennial temple of Ezekiel will be built in Jerusalem by the Master Architect of the World, Jesus Christ.

CHAPTER 15

THE 70TH YEAR OF JUBILEE

The Jews celebrate the seventh day of each week as the Sabbath or rest day. **"Six days you shall labor and do all your work, but the seventh day is the Sabbath of the Lord your God."** (Ex. 20:9-10a, NKJV.)

The Israelites were to make a sacrifice on the first day of each lunar month, i.e., on the conjunction of the moon with the sun or what we refer to as the New Moon. **'At the beginnings of your months you shall present a burnt offering to the Lord.'** (Num. 28:11a.) There are approximately eleven days more in a solar year than in twelve lunar months. To make the length of the lunar year approximately equal to the length of the solar year a thirteenth lunar month has to be added seven times in a nineteen-year cycle.

God instituted the ceremonial calendar when the Israelites left Egypt in c.1449 B.C. **"This month shall be your beginning of months; it shall be the first month of the year to you."** (Ex. 12:2.) The Bible usually refers to the month as the first month, or the second month, or the third month, etc. In fact, the Bible only gives us the name of four months; the first, second, seventh, and eighth. They are Abib, Ziv, Ethanim, and Bul, respectfully. When God gave the Israelites a new calendar this implies that the old New Years day was some other date than Abib 1. Probably the first day of the seventh month since that date was specified by God to be a Sabbath. Ethanim 1 is the beginning of the Jewish civil calendar.

The modern day Hebrew names closely resemble the Babylonian names of their months. The Israelites probably borrowed the Babylonian names after they were captured by the Babylonians in 586 B.C.

The Babylonian and Hebrew months of the lunar calendars along with the original Biblical names in parentheses are given below in Figure 1. The corresponding Gregorian months are shown to the right of the Hebrew names.

No.	Babylonian Calendar	Hebrew Calendar	Gregorian Calendar
1.	Nisanu	Nisan (or Abib, Ex. 13:4)	Mar—Apr
2.	Ayaru	Iyyar (or Ziv, 1 Kings 6:1)	Apr—May
3.	Simanu	Sivan	May—Jun
4.	Du'uzu	Tammuz	Jun—Jul
5.	Abu	Av	Jul—Aug
6.	Ululu	Elul	Aug—Sep
7.	Tashritu	Tishri (or Ethanim, 1 Kings 8:2)	Sep—Oct
8.	Arakhsamna	Heshvan (or Bul, 1 Kings 6:38)	Oct—Nov
9.	Keslimu	Kislev	Nov—Dec
10.	Tebetu	Tevet	Dec—Jan
11.	Shabatu	Shevat	Jan—Feb
12.	Adaru I	Adar I	Feb—Mar
13.	Adaru II	Adar II	(added 7 times in a 19-year cycle)

FIGURE 1

The Jews also celebrate seven festivals during the year. See Leviticus 23. The seven festivals of the ceremonial calendar are shown in Figure 2.

Early spring—	1) Passover	14th day of the first month (Nisan 14)
	2) Feast of Unleavened Bread	15th thru the 21st day of the first month (Nisan 15-21)
	3) Feast of Firstfruits	first day of the week following the Sabbath of Unleavened Bread
Late spring—	4) Feast of Weeks or Pentecost	50 days after the Sabbath of Unleavened Bread
Late summer—	5) Feast of Trumpets or Rosh Hashanah or New Years Day	first day of the seventh month (Tishri 1)
	6) Day of Atonement	tenth day of the seventh month (Tishri 10)
	7) Feast of Tabernacles	15th thru 22nd day of the seventh month (Tishri 15-22)

FIGURE 2

The Israelites were required by God to let the land rest for a year every seven years. The year when they let the land rest was called a Sabbath Year. **And the Lord spoke to Moses on Mount Sinai, saying, "Speak to the children of Israel, and say to them: 'When you come into the land which I give you, then the land shall keep a sabbath to the Lord. Six years you shall sow your field, and six years you shall prune your vineyard, and gather in its fruit; but** in the seventh year there shall be a sabbath of solemn rest for the land, a sabbath to the Lord. You shall neither sow your field nor prune your vineyard. What grows of its own accord of your harvest you shall not reap, nor gather the grapes of your untended vine, for it is a year of rest for the land.'" (Lev. 25:1-5.)

And after every seven Sabbath Years, they were also required to set aside another sabbath year called a Jubilee Year. **'And you shall count seven sabbaths of years for yourself, seven times seven years; and the time of the seven sabbaths of years shall be to you forty-nine years. Then you shall cause the trumpet of the Jubilee to sound on the tenth day of the seventh month; on the Day of Atonement you shall make the trumpet to sound throughout all your land.'** (Lev. 25:8-9.)

The Jubilee Year was the year following the seventh Sabbath Year. Therefore, the jubilee years would be the 50th year, 99th year, 148th year, 197th year, and so forth; or 49x + 1 where x is a cardinal number. **'And you shall consecrate the fiftieth year, and proclaim liberty throughout all the land to all its inhabitants. It shall be a Jubilee for you; and each of you shall return to his possession, and each of you shall return to his family. That fiftieth year shall be a Jubilee to you; in it you shall neither sow nor reap what grows of its own accord, nor gather the grapes of your untended vine. For it is the Jubilee; it shall be holy to you; you shall eat its produce from the field. In this Year of Jubilee, each of you shall return to his possession.'** (Lev. 25:10-13.)

To summarize, I have made a chart of the commands of God with respect to the Sabbath Year and/or the Year of Jubilee. See Figure 3.

God's Command	Sabbath Year	Jubilee Year
start date time of year cycle land rest people property (real estate) public worship	when you come into the land month of Tishri (Sep—Oct) every 7th year neither sow nor reap — — the Law (Torah) read to all (Deut. 31:10)	when you come into the land Tishri 10 every 49th year starting with the 50th year neither sow nor reap liberty to all inhabitants* returned to original possessors —

FIGURE 3

* The Bible (NKJV) defines what 'liberty to all inhabitants' means. If a fellow Hebrew is poor and sells himself to you, you shall not compel him to serve as a slave. He shall serve you until the Year of Jubilee. Then you shall let him go, and his children (Lev. 25:39-46). If a fellow Hebrew is poor and sells himself to a rich sojourner or stranger, he may be redeemed by one of his brothers, or his uncle, or his uncle's son, or one of closest kin. The redemption price

shall be based on the number of years until the Year of Jubilee. In the Year of Jubilee, he and his children shall be released (Lev. 25:47-55).

The Israelites were commanded not to borrow and they were commanded to forgive debts. If a fellow Hebrew owes you a debt, on the seventh year you shall grant a release of debts (Deut. 15:1-23). He has six years of grace to settle the debt. After six years the debt is to be forgiven; i.e., it will be marked off as a bad debt by our method of accounting. [Note: This was to be done every seven years and so it was not just a Sabbath Year requirement.]

If we assume the Israelite exodus out of Egypt was in 1449 B.C. (see Chapter 5, On the Road to The 7th Millennium) and allow for the Israelites wandering in the desert for 40 years and another 5 1/2 years for conquering the land of Canaan we get 1404 B.C. Therefore, we should start counting the sabbath and jubilee years from 1403 B.C.; that is, when they first sowed their fields. This is shown in Figure 4 below.

Jewish Era— A.M.*	Christian Era— B.C./A.D.	Event
2312	1450-1449	Israelites left Egypt after the Passover meal on Nisan 15, 1449 B.C. 40 years in the desert
2352	1410-1409	Israelites entered Canaan on Nisan 10, 1409 B.C. Israel begins conquering the land of Canaan. It took 5 1/2 years.
2353	1409-1408	
2354	1408-1407	
2355	1407-1406	
2356	1406-1405	
2357	1405-1404	
2358	1404-1403	
2359	**1403-1402**	Israel conquered Canaan. Israelites divided up the Promised Land. **Begin counting sabbath and jubilee years.**
2360		
2361	1402-1401	1st full year in control of land, sowing and reaping. (Lev. 25:2-4)
2362	1401-1400	2nd year
2363	1400-1399	3rd year
2364	1399-1398	4th year
2365	1398-1397	5th year
2366	1397-1396	6th year
	1396-1395	1st Sabbath Year
		[From here on count by seven with an immediate insert after every 7th sabbath year for a jubilee year.]
2373		
2380		
2387	1389-1388	2nd Sabbath Year
2394	1382-1381	3rd Sabbath Year
2401	1375-1374	4th Sabbath Year
	1368-1367	5th Sabbath Year
	1361-1360	6th Sabbath Year

2408	1354-1353	7th Sabbath Year
2409	**1353-1352**	**1st Jubilee Year starts Tishri 10, 1353 B.C.**
		89 sabbath years, 8th to 96th Sabbath Years
		2nd to 13th Jubilee Years
	724-723	97th Sabbath Year
	717-716	98th Sabbath Year
	716-715	**14th Jubilee Year**
	710-709	99th Sabbath Year
	703-702	**100th Sabbath Year**
		In Hezekiah's 14th year as King of Judah (702-701 B.C. per Edwin R. Thiele's book, "The Mysterious Numbers of the Hebrew Kings", page 120), Isaiah prophesied no harvest for two years but plenty of food to eat **(II Kings 19:29** and **Isaiah 37:30)**; possibly a sabbath year and jubilee year (see **Leviticus 25** and **Antiquity of the Jews, book 3, chapter 12, section 3**), or more likely, a sabbath year and a year under siege back to back. Neither II Kings nor Isaiah state that one or both years, 3059 A.M. or 3060 A.M., were sabbath years. Jerusalem was under siege by the Assyrians at the time, which means working in the fields was not possible. This figure assumes the second year of no planting or harvesting is due to the siege. [Antiquity of the Jews by Flavius Josephus can be found on Netscape search engine at http://www.earlyjewishwritings.com/josephus.html.]
		76 sabbath years, 101st to 176th Sabbath Years
		15th to 25th Jubilee Years
3038	**164-163**	**177th Sabbath Year**
3045		**re: Antiq. b.12, c.9, s.5 & I Mac. 6:48-54**
3046		I Maccabees states that the Jews were out of stocks
3052		of provisions because it was a sabbath year. This
3059		happened in the 150th year of Seleucid's Era (312 B.C.
		—150 = 162 B.C.). Therefore, the sabbath year must have
3598		occurred the year before 162 B.C. [I Maccabees can be found at http://www.sacred-texts.com/bib/apo/ma1.htm.]
		17 sabbath years, 178th to 194th Sabbath Years
		26th to 27th Jubilee Years
3724	38-37	**195th Sabbath Year**
		re: Antiq. of the Jews, b.14, c.16, s.2

3731	31-30	196th Sabbath Year
3732	**30-29**	**28th Jubilee Year**
3738	**24-23**	**197th Sabbath Year**
		re: Antiq. b.15, c.9, s.1 implies a Sabbath Year
3745	17-16	198th Sabbath Year
3752	10-9	199th Sabbath Year
3759	3-2 B.C.	200th Sabbath Year
3766	5-6 A.D.	201st Sabbath Year
3773	12-13	202nd Sabbath Year
3780	19-20	203rd Sabbath Year
3781	**20-21**	**29th Jubilee Year**
3787	26-27	204th Sabbath Year
3794	33-34	205th Sabbath Year
3801	40-41	206th Sabbath Year
3808	47-48	207th Sabbath Year
3815	54-55	208th Sabbath Year
3822	61-62	209th Sabbath Year
3829	68-69	210th Sabbath Year
3830	**69-70**	**30th Jubilee Year**
		271 sabbath years, 211th to 481st Sabbath Years
		31st to 68th Jubilee Years
5733	1972-1973	482nd Sabbath Year
5740	1979-1980	483rd Sabbath Year
5741	**1980-1981**	**69th Jubilee Year**
5747	1986-1987	484th Sabbath Year
5754	1993-1994	485th Sabbath Year
5761	2000-2001	486th Sabbath Year
5768	2007-2008	487th Sabbath Year
5775	2014-2015	488th Sabbath Year
5782	2021-2022	489th Sabbath Year
5789	2028-2029	490th Sabbath Year
5790	**2029-2030**	**70th Jubilee Year**

* A.M. is the abbreviation for Anno Mundi which means 'from the creation of the world'. Jewish chronology has the creation occurring
on 7 October 3761 B.C. The year 1980 corresponds to the Jewish years 5740-5741 A.M. The Jewish New Year, 1 Tishri 5741 A.M., corresponds to 11 September 1980, and the Jewish year 5741 is the same as 1980-1981. The derivation of the creation date can no longer be accurately traced. It became popular about the 9th century A.D. I believe the Jewish Era has approximately 211-year error in it. This means the world is approximately 211 years older than is specified in the Jewish Era.

FIGURE 4

I believe the 70th Year of Jubilee will be the greatest of all jubilee years. And I believe it will usher in Christ's Millennial Reign. The 70th Year of Jubilee will give liberty to all people. It will be a happy time for all who are going into the new heavens and the new earth (Is.65:17).

There are at least four astounding Scriptural events which lead me to believe that we are close to the Lord's Second Coming.
1. The right time in history—the 7th 'day', or the Sabbath 'Day', or the Sabbath Millennium.
2. Jesus' own prophesy saying that He will be 'perfected' or finished on the third day (Luke 13:32).
3. 'This generation' or the generation that sees all these things fulfilled (Matt. 24:32-35).
4. The 70th Year of Jubilee is the acceptable year of the Lord.

So, if Jesus Christ returns in the year 2029, what is the urgency? Remember, the rapture occurs at least seven years before the Lord's Second Coming. And we do not know when Jesus will call us home to be with Him. Yes, the time is short. **"Seek the Lord while He may be found, Call upon Him while He is near."** (Is. 55:6.)

Jesus told His disciples this parable about Himself. **"Blessed are those servants whom the master** (Jesus)**, when he comes, will find watching. Assuredly, I say to you that he** (Jesus) **will gird himself and have them sit down to eat, and will come and serve them."** (Luke 12:37.)

And the Isaiah passage that Jesus read in the synagogue (Luke 4:18-19) will then be fulfilled completely. **"The Spirit of the Lord God is upon Me, because the Lord has anointed Me to preach good tidings to the poor; He has sent Me to heal the brokenhearted, to proclaim liberty to the captives, and the opening of the prison to those who are bound; to proclaim the acceptable year of the Lord, and the day of vengeance of our God, to comfort all who mourn, to console those who mourn in Zion, to give them beauty for ashes, the oil of joy for mourning, the garment of praise for the spirit of heaviness; that they may be called trees of righteousness, the planting of the Lord, that He may be glorified."** (Is. 61:1-3.)

Now the Lord is the Spirit; and where the Spirit of the Lord is, there is liberty. (2 Cor. 3:17.) Oh Happy Day. Amen.

CHAPTER 16
THE STUDY OF REVELATION

Introduction

Taking the advice of good journalism practice I will start off by reporting on the five w's.

1. Who wrote Revelation? The Apostle John wrote Revelation.

2. What is Revelation? Revelation is the last book in the Christian Bible.

3. Where was Revelation written? On an island between Greece and Turkey called Patmos.

4. When was Revelation written? It was written about A.D. 100.

5. Why was Revelation written? Because God wanted it written so that His people would know how this age ends.

The book of Revelation is more accurately called The Revelation of Jesus Christ, as it was given to the Apostle John. Revelation was penned by John who was told by Jesus Christ to write and what to write.

The word revelation is synonymous with apocalypse. Some Bibles have the book of Revelation called The Apocalypse of Jesus Christ. Other variants with the word revelation or apocalypse in the title can also be found.

It is estimated to have been written in A.D. 96 when John was an old man while in prison on the island of Patmos.

Some theologian scholars would like for you to believe that John wrote Revelation in veiled language because he was afraid to tell you the facts for fear that the Roman government would chop off his head. I don't believe this. First, the message is from Jesus Christ, not John. Therefore, they would have to be saying God is afraid of what harm would come to John as a result of his penning this message.—Afraid?—I don't think so. Besides, John is an old man, in his late 80's or early 90's as a minimum. I think John would have welcomed death since all the original disciples were already martyred for their faith and were with their Lord.

Revelation can be divided up into three parts from two separate perspectives; the past, the present, and the future from a) around A.D. 100 when the book was written, and b) from our present day perspective. See Figure 1 below.

From the Apostle John's Viewpoint: Past— Present— Future—	Revelation Chapter 1 Revelation Chapters 2 and 3 Revelation Chapters 4 through 22
From Our Present Day Viewpoint: Past— Past and Present, up to the rapture— Future (post rapture)—	Revelation Chapter 1 Revelation Chapters 2 through 6:11 Revelation Chapters 6:12 through 22

Figure 1: Different Perspectives of the Book of Revelation

First, I will discuss the past, present, and future from John's viewpoint.

Jesus tells John in verse 19 of Chapter 1, **"Write the things which you have seen** [past]**, and the things which are** [present]**, and the things which will take place after this** [future]**."** Chapter 4:1 starts off with **"After these things . . ."** indicating future events. Thus, the book of Revelation can be divided into **'things'** of the past, present, and future.

And for this reason many traditional pre-millennial thinkers have the rapture occurring at Rev. 4:1 when it states, **"Come up here, and I will show you things which must take place after this."** [NKJV] The idea is that John experiences the rapture when Jesus says, **"Come up here . . . ."** Christians will experience the rapture, this is true. But, I don't believe that Revelation 4:1 is where the rapture occurs in Revelation.

I used to favor the tradtional approach to the rapture. I believed in a sudden and almost secretive rapture, as hinted at in Isaiah 57:1. I no longer subscribe to a 'stealthy rapture'. The resurrection of all Christians will be one of the most heralded events in all of cosmic occurrences. It compares to Noah's flood, and to Jesus Christ's birth, life, death, and resurrection 2000 years ago. I was convinced after reading a book called Earthquake Resurrection written by David W. Lowe in 2005. [An introduction to the book can be found at <http://www.earthquakeresurrection. com>.] The great earthquake which is described in Rev. 6:12 through 6:16 as so great that **'every mountain and island was moved out of its place'.** (NKJV)

Now from our present day viewpoint.

Chapters 2 and 3 are telling us about the seven types of churches in the world which are identified by Ephesus, Smyrna, Pergamos, Thyatira, Sardis, Philadelphia, and Laodicea. I would hope my earthly church is similar to the one described as the faithful church of Philadelphia. I suspect our earthly churches are some of each. All church members are members of one of these types of seven churches at any given time.

Chapters 4, 5, and the first part of 6 tells us what John would experience while he was transitioning from this life (the present) to the next life (the future).

The first five seals (Rev. 6:1 through Rev. 6:11) which Christ breaks open are the past 1900 years of history and present day occurrences. There have been and will continue to be wars, fighting, conquering or being conquered, killing or being killed, famines, death, and catastrophes since the first century. Has one-fourth of the world's population died as a result of these calamities over the last 1900 years? Yes, I think so. The four riders on the four horses are riding through history.

The sixth and seventh seals have not been broken yet, as of June 2007, by Jesus Christ.

Summary Outline

Figure 2 summarizes the events of Chapters 4 through 19 of Revelation. The summary outline starts with John's perception of the future events that will take place. Chapter 4 through Chapter 19 are the most difficult to decipher and to understand. Basically, Chapter 4 through Chapter 11 are sequential occurrences of the end time events. Revelation 11:19 takes us up to the Lord's Second Coming.

In Chapters 12 through 18, there are seven further embellishments of these end time events. Then it ends with Jesus Christ's return to earth in Revelation 19:1 through Revelation 20:3.

Chapter 20:4-10 is the one thousand year reign of Christ on earth. This is what is referred to as the millennial period or the millennial age.

Chapter 20:11-15 describes God's Judgment Day or what is referred to as the 'Great White Throne Judgment.'

Chapters 21 and 22 give to us a taste what heaven is like. It is a welcome sight after going through what this world has to offer. All the pain, sorrow, tribulation, and death that is lurking in this world. We can appreciate and gladly await Jesus' words, **"Surely, I am coming quickly."**

The above outline is further defined by the figures shown in Figure 5 and Figure 6.

Figure 2: Future Events

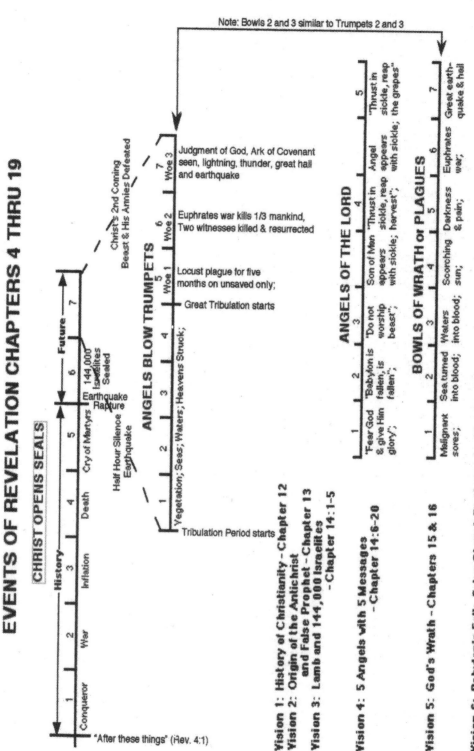

Figure 3: A Summary Outline of the Events in Revelation 6 through 22

Christ Opens Seals	
I) History	
Seal 1	Rider on White Horse goes out to Conqueror
Seal 2	Rider on Red Horse goes out to make War
Seal 3	Rider on Black Horse goes out to cause Inflation and Starvation
Seal 4	Rider on Pale Horse goes out to kill and bring Death to all and Hades to some
Seal 5	Cry of the Martyrs to God to Judge
II) Future	
Seal 6	**Great Worldwide Earthquake & Rapture**; 144,000 Israelites sealed
Seal 7	Seven angels given 7 trumpets to blow [**Tribulation Period Starts; Israel and** <u>Antichrist</u> **sign the covenant (Dan. 9:27)**]
Angels Blow Trumpets	
Trumpet 1	one-third of trees & all green grass burned up
Trumpet 2	one-third of seas became blood & one-third of ships destroyed
Trumpet 3	one-third of river & spring water made bitter
Trumpet 4	one-third of the sun, moon, and stars darkened
Trumpet 5—Woe 1	Satan falls to earth & given permission to release demons from bottomless pit [**Great Tribulation Starts; Antichrist breaks covenant**]
Trumpet 6—Woe 2	one-third of mankind killed by a 200,000,000 demonic army; two witnesses prophesy; witnesses were killed and lay dead for 3 1/2 days, and were resurrected by God; a great earthquake occurred the same hour; 7000 men are killed
Trumpet 7—Woe 3	the kingdom proclaimed, the temple of God was opened and the ark of covenant was seen. There were lightnings, noises, thunderings, an earthquake, and great hail; Christ returns to earth and defeats the <u>Antichrist</u> and his armies
Explanatory Visions	
Vision 1	pageant of the <u>history of Jesus</u> Christ and the Messianic and Christian faith
Vision 2	the characteristics and the origin of the Antichrist and False Prophet
Vision 3	the sealed 144,000 Israelites praise God and the Lamb
Vision 4	declaration of evangelistic messages
Angels of the Lord	Fear God and give glory Him, for the hour of His judgment has come
Angel 1 speaks	Babylon is fallen, is fallen, that great city, because she has made all
Angel 2 speaks	nations drunk

Angel 3 speaks	If anyone worships the beast &his image, & receives his mark will drink the wrath of God
	Jesus appeared on a white cloud with a sharp sickle
Angel 4 speaks	Thrust in Your sickle & reap, for the time has come for You to reap the harvest of saved
Angel 5 speaks	Thrust in Your sharp sickle & gather the clusters of the vine for the grapes are fully ripe of the unsaved
Vision 5	God's wrath is expressed with seven last plagues
Bowls of Wrath of God	
Bowl 1	malignant sores on men who had the mark of the beast and/or worshiped his image
Bowl 2	the sea turns to blood and every living creature in the sea died
Bowl 3	the waters of the rivers and springs turn to blood
Bowl 4	men are scorched with great heat
Bowl 5	the beast kingdom became dark
Bowl 6	the Euphrates River dried up preparing the way for the kings of the east to gather at Armageddon
Bowl 7	a mighty and great worldwide earthquake where every island and mountain disappeared
Vision 6	Babylon the great is fallen, is fallen: false religions (churches) are destroyed
Vision 7	Babylon, that mighty city is fallen: world economy and commerce are destroyed
Christ's 2nd Coming	Christ returns with His army of saints. He destroys all of His enemies. Cast the Antichrist and False Prophet into the lake of fire and binds up Satan and throws him into the bottomless pit for 1000 years
Christ's Millennial Reign	Saints reign with Christ for 1000 years. After 1000 years Satan is released. He deceives many from all over the world to follow him. Satan battles God in the great Gog and Magog war. God defeats Satan and his followers. God throws Satan into the lake of fire where the Antichrist & False Prophet are.
God's Judgment Day	God judges all people of the world. The Book of Life was opened to see if Jesus Christ has a persons name in it, or if it has been blotted out. If it is blotted out other books are opened to see if person has sinned. [All men are sinners and God will by no means clear the guilty.] Anyone not found written in the Book of Life will be cast into the lake of fire. Death and Hades are also cast into the lake of fire.
Eternity Described	God creates a new heaven and a new earth. It will last forever. There is no death, nor sorrow, nor crying, nor any pain. There is no darkness and no need for a sun, nor a moon, nor any stars because Jesus Christ supplies the new world its light.

Throne of God

The throne of God is described in Revelation 4. I attempted to make a figure that described the throne and the characters surrounding the throne. [It doesn't come close in doing God's Throne justice.] See Figure 4. We probably all have some questions about the characters; especially God, the angels, the four living creatures, and the elders. Nobody has seen God, but many people have seen Jesus Christ in His day. When Jesus walked on earth I believe that He probably looked like most men his age.

Some people have seen angels. They probably look a lot like men. No surprise there, but with spiritual features. They appear 'out of nowhere' and vanish 'into thin air' very fast.

I believe the four living creatures have the features that John described to them in Revelation. These are probably special creatures that were created by God for the express purpose of serving the Lord in the way as seen in Revelation. The four living creatures discussed in Ezekiel Chapter 1 are similar but different than these. The creatures in Ezekiel have four wings and these have six.

The twenty-four elders, we assume, are twenty-four Biblical patriarchs. Mainly, because there were twelve sons of Jacob and twelve disciples of Jesus. But, Judas is in hell. So, eleven of the original disciples plus the apostle Paul, gives us the necessary twelve apostles.—I don't think so. Why? Because the twelve sons of Jacob and the twelve apostles of Jesus haven't been resurrected yet. They haven't been given a glorified body yet. Remember, Christ was the first fruit from the dead.

I don't know who the four living creatures are, or who the elders are, or even, who the angels are.

Figure 4: Throne of God

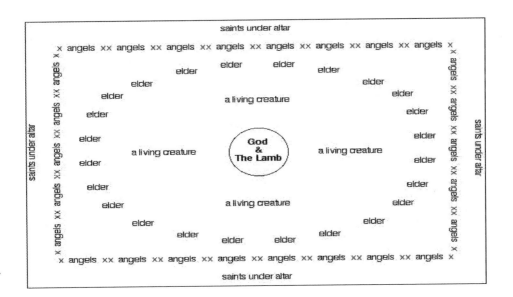

Characters in Revelation (NKJV)

Those who are or will be in HEAVEN
- —God Father
- —Jesus
- —Holy Spirit (7 Spirits of God)
- —John, the apostle and author of Revelation
- —4 living creatures
- —24 elders
- —martyrs of the Lord
- —multitudes of believers or saints
- —12 tribes of Israel (non-verbal)
- —12 apostles of Jesus (non-verbal)
- —7 churches of Asia Minor (non-verbal)
- —144,000 Israelites (non-verbal)
- —2 witnesses (non-verbal)
- —the archangel, Michael, and his angels (non-verbal)
- —7 angels of the 7 churches (non-verbal)
- —7 angels blowing the 7 trumpets (non-verbal)
- —7 angels with 7 bowls of plagues
- —5 angels with 5 messages from God

Those who are or will be in HELL or HADES
- —Satan
- —Antichrist
- —False Prophet
- —1/3 of angelic beings
- —multitudes of demons
- —multitudes of unbelievers

Symbolism used in Revelation

Symbols are used in prophesy to emphasize the truths in the Bible. Especially, in the apocalyptic books of Daniel and Revelation. Symbols can be divided into two categories, There are 'good' symbols and 'bad' or 'evil' symbols, whether they are portraying something that is good or from God, or something that is worldly, demonic, or of Satan. Some of the more common symbols used in the book of Revelation are shown in Figure 5.

'Good' Symbols	
Jesus Christ	Alpha and Omega; Beginning and End; First and Last; Son of Man; Son of God; Amen; Faithful and True Witnesses; Beginning of the creation of God; Lion of the tribe of Judah; the Root of David; the Lamb; another mighty angel; male Child of woman (Israel); Lord of lords; King of kings; Faithful and True; a name written that no one knew except Himself; The Word of God; who is and who was and who is to come.
church	moon under woman's feet; the Lamb's bride
churches	lampstands
the nation Israel	woman who bore the male Child
12 tribes of Israel	garland of 12 stars on head of woman
Jerusalem	Sodom; Egypt; great city; great city where our Lord was crucified; great Babylon
new Jerusalem	holy Jerusalem; great city; two lampstand
two witnesses	two olive trees; two lampstands
saints	white cloud; armies in heaven, clothed in fine linen; white and clean
the saved (believers)	harvest of the earth; multitudes from all nations; tribes, peoples and tongues clothed in white robes.
angels	stars in heaven
sea (waters)	all nations; peoples; multitudes, nations; tongues (refer to Rev. 13:1).
earth (land)	the nation Israel (as referred to in Rev. 13:11).
'Evil' Symbols	
Satan	dragon; fiery red dragon; serpent; devil; great star fallen from heaven; king over locusts (or scorpions); angel of bottomless pit; Wormwood; Abaddon; Apollyon.
human beings (leaders/rulers)	riders on white, red, black, and pale horses

hell	the beast; scarlet beast [John refers to the Antichrist in other of his writings; 1 John 2:18 & 4:3]
Antichrist	2nd beast; lamb with two horns
False Prophet	Babylon; <u>Babylon the great</u>; scarlet woman; mother of harlots
false church	Babylon; great city Babylon
economic/commerce	locusts from the abyss; scorpions
demons	cluster of grapes
unsaved	1/3 of the stars cast out of heaven
fallen angels	

Figure 5: Good/Evil Symbols in Revelation

Symbol Analyses In Revelation

Figures 6a and 6b show a comprehensive discussion of these events as seen by John the revelator and relevant for our day, that is, from Revelation Chapter 1 up to eternity. A thorough outline is shown in Figures 6a and 6b. Figure 6a goes up to Jesus Christ's Second Coming, i.e., Rev. 1:1 through Rev. 11:19. Figure 6b goes from Rev. 12:1 all the way to the end of Revelation.

The symbols are usually listed in the right column along with the Bible passage or passages it was taken from. The person, place, or thing that the symbol is talking about is in the left-hand column opposite the symbol. Sometimes the left-hand column has the person (or voice) who said what is in the right-hand column.

[The symbols were taken from the New King James Version of the Bible. The symbols will be somewhat different in different versions of the Bible.]

Figure 6a: Symbol Analyses - Part 1

Chapter 1	Chapter 1
Jesus Christ	the Alpha and the Omega (Rev. 1:8 & 1:11)
	the Beginning and the End (Rev. 1:8)
	the First and the Last (Rev. 1:11)
—a loud voice	—as of a trumpet (Rev. 1:10)
—the voice	—that spoke to me (Rev. 1:12)
—His voice	—as the sound of many waters (Rev. 1:15)
Jesus Christ	the Son of Man (Rev. 1:13-16)
—head and hair	—white like wool
—eyes	—like a flame of fire
—feet	—like fine brass
—voice	—as the sound of many waters
—in right hand	—were seven stars
—out of mouth	—went a sharp two-edged sword
—countenance	—like the sun shining in its strength
seven angels	seven stars of the seven golden lampstands(Rev. 1:20)
seven churches	seven golden lampstands(Rev. 1:20)
Chapter 2	**Chapter 2**
Jesus Christ	He who holds the seven stars in His right hand
	He who walks in the midst of the seven golden lampstands (Rev. 2:1)
Jesus Christ	the First and the Last (Rev. 2:8)
???	(tribulation ten days) (Rev. 2:10)
Jesus Christ	He who has the sharp two-edged sword (Rev. 2:12)
Jesus Christ	Son of God (Rev. 2:18)
—eyes	—like a flame of fire
—feet	—like fine brass
???	(great tribulation) (Rev. 2:22)
Chapter 3	**Chapter 3**
Jesus Christ	He who has the seven Spirits of God and seven stars (Rev. 3:1)
	He who will not blot out his (your) name from the Book of Life (3:5)
Jesus Christ	He who has the key of David, who opens & no one shuts, shuts and no one opens (3:7)

	He who will you keep from the hour of trial which shall come upon the whole world (3:10)
Jesus Christ	Amen (Rev. 3:14) Faithful and True Witness (Rev. 3:14) the Beginning of the creation of God (Rev. 3:14)
Chapter 4 voice of God	**Chapter 4** like a trumpet speaking with me (John) saying, "Come up here, and I will show you things which must take place after this." (Rev. 4:1, refer to Rev. 1:10)
—God sat on throne —around God's throne	—like a jasper and a sardius stone in appearance (Rev. 4:3) —a rainbow like an emerald (Rev. 4:3)
24 elders around God	24 elders sat on 24 thrones clothed in white robes and with gold crowns on their heads worships God and cast their crowns before the throne of God (Rev. 4:4, 10)
from God's throne	proceeded lightnings, thundering, and voices (Rev. 4:5)
seven Spirits of God	seven lamps of fire are seven Spirits of God before the throne of God (Rev. 4:5)
—sea of glass	—like crystal
four living creatures	in the midst and around God's throne are 4 living creatures full of eyes in front and in back (Rev. 4:6-7)
—first living creature —second living creature —third living creature —fourth living creature	—like a lion —like a calf —face like a man —like a flying eagle
4 living creatures	do not rest day or night, saying, "Holy, holy, holy, Lord God Almighty, who was and is and is to come!" (Rev. 4:8)
24 elders	cast their crowns before the throne, saying, "You are worthy, O Lord, to receive glory and honor and power; for You created all things, and by Your will they exist and were created." (Rev. 4:11)
Chapter 5 God's right hand	**Chapter 5** in the right hand of Him who sat on the throne was a scroll sealed with seven seals (5:1)
strong angel	a strong angel proclaiming with a loud voice, "Who is worthy to open the scroll and to loose its seals?" (Rev. 5:2)

one of the elders	said to me (John), "Do not weep. Behold, the Lion of the tribe of Judah, the Root of David, has prevailed to open the scroll and to loose its seven seals." (Rev. 5:5)
Jesus Christ —<u>seven Spirits of God</u>	Lamb having seven horns and seven eyes which are seven Spirits of God sent out into all the earth (Rev. 5:6) —seven horns and seven eyes
Jesus Christ	He (the Lamb) came and took the scroll out of the right hand of Him (God) who sat on the throne (Rev. 5:8)
elders & creatures	the four living creatures and the twenty-four elders sang a new song, saying: "You are worthy to take the scroll, and to open its seal; for You were slain, and have redeemed us to God by Your blood out of every tribe and tongue and people and nation, and have made us kings and priests to our God; and we shall reign on the earth." (Rev. 5:9-10)
angelic hosts	the voice of many angels around the throne, the living creatures, and the elders saying, "Worthy is the Lamb who was slain to receive power and riches and wisdom, and strength and honor and glory and blessing!" (Rev. 5:11-12)
every creature	which is in heaven and on the earth and under the earth and such as are in the sea, saying, 'Blessing and honor and glory and power be to Him who sits on the throne and to the Lamb, forever and ever!" (5:13)
Chapter 6 **Jesus opens 1st seal** 1st living creature saying —white horse & rider	**Chapter 6** **Jesus opens 1st seal** heard one of the 4 living creatures saying with a voice like thunder, "Come and see." (6:1) —conquering and to be conquered on earth (Rev. 6:2)
Jesus opens 2nd seal 2nd living creature saying —red horse & rider	the second living creature saying, "Come and see." (Rev. 6:3) —war on earth (Rev. 6:4)
Jesus opens 3rd seal 3rd living creature saying —black horse & rider	the third living creature saying, "Come and see." (Rev. 6:5) —inflation and starvation on earth (Rev. 6:5)
voice of God	a voice in midst of the 4 living creatures saying, "A quart of wheat for a denarius, and three quarts of barley for a denarius; and do not harm the oil and the wine." (Rev. 6:6)

Jesus opens 4th seal 4th living creature saying —pale horse & rider	the fourth living creature saying, "Come and see." (Rev. 6:7) —the rider was called Death and Hades and was given power to 'them' to kill with sword, with hunger, or by beasts 1/4 of people on earth (Rev. 6:8)
Jesus opens 5th seal martyrs under altar	martyrs cried with a loud voice, saying, "How long, O Lord, holy and true, until You judge and avenge our blood on those who dwell on the earth?" (Rev. 6:9-10) **['under the altar' would indicate the saints have not been raised yet]**
Jesus opens 6th seal great worldwide earthquake Satan & his angels fall to earth	every mountain & island moved out of its place **[worldwide earthquake rapture?]** stars of heaven fell to earth like a fig tree dropping its late figs (Rev. 6:12-14)
Chapter 7 4 corners angels	**Chapter 7** standing at the 4 corners of the earth, holding the 4 winds of the earth (Rev. 7:1)
Jesus Christ	another angel [Christ?] ascending from the east, having the seal of the living God cried with a loud voice to the four angels to harm the earth and the sea, saying, "Do not harm the earth, the sea, or the trees till we [Father and Son?] have sealed the servants of our God on their foreheads." (Rev. 7:2-3)
144,000 sealed Israelites	12,000 sealed Christian believers from each tribe of Israel; they were sealed on their foreheads (Rev. 7:4-8)
the saved (saints)	a great multitude of all nations, tribes, people, and tongues, standing before the Lamb, clothed with white robes cried out with a loud voice, saying, "Salvation belongs to our God who sits on the throne, and to the Lamb!" (Rev.7:9-10) **[Note: the saints are in heaven now, clothed with white robes.]**
heavenly hosts	all the angels, elders, and 4 living creatures stood around God's throne, and fell on their faces before the throne and worshiped God, saying, "Amen! Blessing and glory wisdom, thanksgiving and honor and power and might, be to our God forever and ever. Amen." (Rev. 7:11-12)
one of the elders	answered, saying, to me (John), "Who are these arrayed in white robes, and where did they come from?" (Rev. 7:13)
John	said to the elder, "Sir, you know." (Rev. 7:14)
one of the elders	the elder said to me (John), "These are the ones who come out of the

great tribulation and washed their robes and made them white in the blood of the Lamb. Therefore they are before the throne of God, and serve Him day and night in His temple. And He who sits on the throne will dwell among them. They shall neither hunger anymore nor thirst anymore; the sun shall not strike them, nor any heat; for the Lamb who is in the midst of the throne will shepherd them and lead them to living fountains of waters. God will wipe every tear from their eyes."
(Rev. 7:14-17)

Chapter 8 **Jesus opens** <u>7th seal</u> silence for about1/2 hour	**Chapter 8** **Jesus opens 7th seal** **Tribulation Period starts?? [signing of covenant between** **Israel and Antichrist (Dan. 9:27]**
7 angels stand before God	7 angels given 7 trumpets (Rev. 8:2)
another angel with censer	filled with incense and prayers of the saints thrown down to earth causing noises, thunderings, lightnings, and an earthquake (8:3-5)
1st angel blows trumpet	hail and fire mingled with blood thrown to earth; 1/3 of trees burned up and all green grass burned up. (Rev. 8:7)
2nd angel blows trumpet	something like a great mountain burning with fire thrown into the sea; 1/3 of the living creatures in the sea die; 1/3 of the ships destroyed (Rev. 8:8-9)
3rd angel blows trumpet	a great star falls from heaven, burning like a torch and fell on 1/3 of the rivers and springs; waters became bitter; many men die (8:10-11)
4th angel blows trumpet	1/3 of sun darkened; 1/3 of the moon and stars darkened; 1/3 of the day and night shortened; a flying angel said, "Woe, woe, woe to the inhabitants of the earth, because of the remaining blasts of the trumpet of the three angels who are about to sound!" (Rev. 8:12-13)
Chapter 9 **5th angel blows** **trumpet—Woe 1** Satan kicked out of heaven	**Chapter 9** **5th angel blows** **trumpet—Woe 1** a star fallen from heaven to earth & he was given key to the bottomless pit (hell). (9:1-2)
demons released from hell	locusts (demons) came out of hell upon earth & commanded not to harm the green grass on earth nor any men who have the <u>seal of God</u> on their foreheads. The locusts were authority to torment but not to

	kill for 5 months. (Rev. 9:3-10) **[Christ preached to these spirits; see 1 Pet. 3:18-19 and 2 Pet. 2:4]**
—power	—like scorpions
—shape	—like horses prepared for battle
—faces	—like faces of men
—hair	—like women's hair
—teeth	—like lion's teeth
—breastplates	—like breastplates of iron
—sound of wings	—like sound of chariots with horses running into battle
—tails	—like scorpions tails with stings
demon's king (Satan) called	in Hebrew is <u>Abaddon</u> and in Greek is Apollyon (Rev. 9:11)
6th angel blows trumpet—Woe 2 voice from 4 horns of the golden altar which is before God	saying to the 6th angel who had the trumpet, "Release the four angels who are bound at the great river Euphrates.' "The four angels (demons?) were released to kill 1/3 of mankind by fire, smoke, and brimstone which came out of their mouths. The size of their army was 200,000,000 (Rev. 9:13-19)
<u>**Chapter 10**</u> Jesus Christ	<u>**Chapter 10**</u> another mighty angel coming down from heaven, clothed with a cloud, with a rainbow on his head, his face like the sun, and his feet like pillars of fire. (Rev. 10:1)
Jesus Christ	he had a little book open, in his hand; his right foot on the sea and his left foot on the land. He cried with a loud voice; 7 thunders uttered their voices. (Rev. 10:2-3)
a voice from heaven	I, John, was about to write but a voice from heaven said to me, John, "Seal up the things which the seven thunders uttered, and do not write them." (Rev. 10:4)
Jesus Christ	the angel whom I, John, saw standing on the sea and on the land lifted up his hand to heaven and swore by Him (God) who lives forever and ever that there should be delay no longer and the mystery of God would be finished before the 7th angel blows his trumpet. (10:5-7)
a voice from heaven	the voice which I, John, heard from heaven spoke to me again and said, "Go take the little book which is open in the hand of the angel who stands on the sea and on the earth." (Rev. 10:8)
John	went to the angel and said to him, "Give me the little book." (Rev. 10:9)
Jesus Christ	and He said to me (John), "Take and eat it; and it will make your stomach bitter, but it will be as sweet as honey in your mouth." (10:9)

Jesus Christ	and He said to me (John), "You must prophesy again about many peoples, nations, tongues, and kings." (Rev. 10:11)
Chapter 11 Jesus Christ	**Chapter 11** angel stood, saying, "Rise and measure the temple of God, the altar, and those who worship there. But leave out the court which is outside the temple, and do not measure it, for it has been given to the Gentiles. And they will tread the holy city under foot for forty-two months. And I will give power to my two witnesses, and they will prophesy one thousand two hundred and sixty days, clothed in sackcloth." (11:1-3)
—reed	—like a measuring rod
two witnesses (Enoch & Elijah)	two olive trees & two lampstands standing before the God of the earth (Rev. 11:4) —fire proceeds from their mouth to destroy those that would harm them (Rev. 11:5) —have power to shut heaven; no rain, turn waters into blood; strike earth with all plagues as often as they desire (Rev. 11:6)
Antichrist	the beast that ascends out of hell and will kill the two witnesses (11:7)
Jerusalem	their dead bodies will lie in the street of the great city called Sodom and Egypt where our Lord was crucified (Rev. 11:8)
voice from heaven	after 3 1/2 days the breath of life from God entered them, and loud voice from heaven said, "Come up here."; the two witnesses ascended to heaven; in the same hour there was a great earthquake and 1/10 of the city fell and 7000 men killed (Rev. 11:11-13) **[another earthquake with a resurrection]**
7th angel blows trumpet—Woe 3 loud voices in heaven	loud voices in heaven, saying, "The kingdoms of this world have become the kingdoms of our Lord and of His Christ, and He shall reign forever and ever!" (Rev. 11:15)
24 elders	the twenty-four elders who sat before God on their thrones fell on their faces and worshiped God, saying: "We give You thanks, O Lord God Almighty, the One who is and who was and who is to come, because You have taken Your great power and reigned. The nations were angry, and Your wrath has come, and the time of the dead, that they should be judged, and that You should reward Your servants the prophets and the saints, and those who fear Your name, small and great, and should destroy those who destroy the earth." (11:16-18)
temple of God	the temple of God was opened in heaven, and the ark of His covenant was seen in His temple. There were lightnings, noises, thunderings, an earthquake, and great hail (Rev. 11:19).

Figure 6b: Symbol Analyses - Part 2

Chapter 12	Chapter 12
Vision 1	**Vision 1**
the nation of Israel	woman clothed with the sun (God's glory) (Rev. 12:1)
—church	—moon under woman's (Israel's) feet
—12 tribes	—on head a garland of 12 stars
Jesus Christ	Israel bears a male Child with much labor and pain (Rev. 12:2)
Satan	fiery red dragon with 7 heads and 7 diadems on his heads, and 10 horns (Rev. 12:3)
—tail of dragon	—influence of Satan
fallen angels	1/3 of the stars of heaven cast out of heaven (Rev. 12:4)
Satan	dragon, serpent, the devil (Rev. 12:9)
a <u>heavenly voice</u>	a loud voice saying in heaven, "Now salvation, and strength, and the kingdom of our God, and the power of His Christ have come, for the accuser of our brethren, who accused them before our God day and night, has been cast down. And they overcame him by the blood of the Lamb and by the word of their testimony, and they did not love their lives to the death. Therefore rejoice, O heavens, and you who dwell in them! Woe to the inhabitants of the earth and the sea! For the devil has come down to you, having great wrath, because he knows that he has a short time." (Rev. 12:10-12).
the nation Israel	woman given two wings of a great eagle that she might fly into the wilderness to her place, where she is nourished for a time and times and half a time, from the presence of the serpent. (Rev. 12:14)
Satan	serpent spewed water out of his mouth (told lies), but the earth (Petra???) protected the woman (Israel) and he made war on the rest of her offspring, who keep the commandments of God and have the testimony of Jesus Christ. (Rev. 12:15-17)
Chapter 13	**Chapter 13**
Vision 2	**Vision 2**
all nations	the sea (waters) (Rev. 13:1)
Antichrist	1st beast having 7 heads and 10 horns, and on his horns10 crowns, and on his heads a blasphemous name (Rev. 13:1-2)
—1st beast	—like a leopard
—feet	—like the feet of a bear
—mouth	—like a mouth of a lion
—power & authority	—from Satan

Satan	dragon (Rev. 13:3)
Antichrist	one of the beast's heads as if it had been mortally wounded, and his deadly wound was healed (Rev. 13:3)
the world	And all the world marveled and followed the beast (antichrist). So they worshiped the dragon (Satan) who gave authority to the beast; and they worshiped the beast, saying, "Who is like the beast? Who is able to make war with him?" And he was given a mouth speaking great things and blasphemies, and he was given authority to continue for forty-two months. Then he opened his mouth in blasphemy against God, to blaspheme His name, His tabernacle, and those who dwell in heaven. And it was granted to him to make war with the saints and to overcome them. And authority was given him over every tribe, tongue, and nation. (Rev. 13:3-7).
the nation of Israel	the earth (land) (Rev. 13:11)
False Prophet —two horns —spoke	2nd beast (Rev. 13:11-16, refer to Rev. 16:13) —like a lamb (he sounds like Jesus) —like a dragon (Satan)
False Prophet False Prophet	exercises all the authority of 1st beast in his presence, and causes the earth and those who dwell in it to worship the 1st beast, whose deadly wound was healed. He performs great signs, so that he even makes fire come down from heaven on the earth in the sight of men. And he deceives those who dwell on the earth by those signs which he was granted to do in the sight of the beast, telling those who dwell on the earth to make an image to the beast who was wounded by the sword and lived. (Rev. 13:12-14)
	he (false prophet) was granted power to give breath to the image of the beast, that the image of the beast should both speak and cause as many as would not worship the image of the beast to be killed. And he causes all, both small and great, rich and poor, free and slave, to receive a mark on their right hand or on their foreheads, and that no one may buy or sell except one who has the mark or the name of the beast, or the number of his name. The number of the beast is 666. (Rev. 13:15-18)
Chapter 14 **Vision 3** Jesus Christ	**Chapter 14** **Vision 3** a Lamb (Rev. 14:1)
a <u>heavenly voice</u>	a voice from heaven, like the voice of many waters, and like the voice of loud thunder (14:2)

144,000 Israelites	first-fruits to God and to Jesus Christ (Rev. 14:4)
Angel 1 speaks	another angel flying in the midst of heaven saying with a loud voice, "Fear God and give glory to Him, for the hour of His judgment has come; and worship Him who made heaven and earth, the sea and springs of water." (Rev. 14:6-7)
Angel 2 speaks	another angel followed, saying, "Babylon is fallen, is fallen, that great city, because she has made all nations drink of the wine of the wrath of her fornication." (Rev. 14:8)
Angel 3 speaks	third angel followed them, saying with a loud voice, "If anyone worships the beast and his image, and receives his mark on his forehead or on his hand, he himself shall also drink of the wine of the wrath of God, which is poured out full strength into the cup of His indignation. And he shall be tormented with fire and brimstone in the presence of the holy angels and in the presence of the Lamb. And the smoke of their torment ascends forever and ever; and they have no rest day or night, who worship the beast and his image, and whoever receives the mark of his name." (Rev. 14:9-10)
a heavenly voice	a voice from heaven saying to me (John), "Write: 'Blessed are the dead who die in the Lord from now on.'" "Yes," says the Spirit, "that they may rest from their labors, and their works follow them." (14:13)
Jesus Christ —white cloud —words spoken —reap —harvest —clusters of grapes —great winepress —blood	One like the Son of Man (Rev. 14:14) —holy —out of His mouth went a sharp two-edged sword —judgment —saved —unsaved —hell or the wrath of God —lack of blood or life (death)
Angel 4 speaks	another angel came out of the temple, crying with a loud voice to Him who sat on the cloud, "Thrust in Your sickle and reap, for the time has come for You to reap, for the harvest of the earth is ripe." (Rev.14:15)
another angel (Jesus Christ?)	another angel came out of the temple which is in heaven, he also having a sharp sickle. (Rev. 14:17)
Angel 5 speaks	another angel came out from the altar, who had power over fire, and he cried with a loud cry to him who had the sharp sickle, saying, "Thrust in your sharp sickle and gather the clusters of the vine of the earth, for her grapes are fully ripe" (Rev. 14:18)

Chapter 15	**Chapter 15**
Vision 5	Vision 5
seven angels	having the seven last plagues, for in them the wrath of God is complete (15:1)
Jesus Christ	Lamb (Rev. 15:3)
tribulation martyrs	And they sing the song of Moses, the servant of God, and the song of the Lamb, saying, "Great and marvelous are Your works, Lord God Almighty! Just and true are Your ways, O King of the saints! Who shall not fear You, O Lord, and glorify Your name? For You alone are holy. For all nations shall come and worship before You, for Your judgments have been manifested." (Rev. 15:3-4)
temple	of the tabernacle of the testimony of heaven was opened (Rev. 15:5)
Chapter 16	**Chapter 16**
voice from temple	a loud voice from the temple saying to the seven angels, "Go and pour out the bowls of the wrath of God on the earth." (Rev. 16:1)
Seven Last Plagues	**Seven Last Plagues**
Bowl 1	the first angel poured out his bowl upon the earth, and a foul and loathsome sore came upon men who had the mark of the beast and those who worshiped his image (16:2)
Bowl 2	the second angel poured out his bowl upon the sea, and it became as blood as of a dead man and every living creature of the sea died (Rev. 16:3)
Bowl 3	the third angel poured out his bowl upon the rivers and springs of waters and they became blood (Rev. 16:4)
Bowl 4	the fourth angel poured out his bowl upon the sun, and power was given to him to scorch men with fire (Rev. 16:8)
Bowl 5	the fifth angel poured out his bowl on the throne of the beast, and his kingdom became full of darkness, and they gnawed their tongues because of the pain (Rev. 16:10)
Bowl 6	the sixth angel poured out his bowl on the on the great river Euphrates, and its water was dried up, so that the way of the kings from the east. I, John, saw three unclean spirits like frogs coming out of mouths of Satan, Antichrist, and the False Prophet. These spirits of demons are able to perform signs which go out to the kings of the earth and of the whole world, to gather them to the battle at Armageddon (16:12)

Bowl 7

the seventh angel poured out his bowl into the air, and a loud voice came out of the <u>temple of heaven</u>, from the throne, saying, "It is done!" There were noises, thunderings, lightnings, and the greatest earthquake ever. The great city (Jerusalem) was divided into three parts, and the cities of the nations were destroyed. The great Babylon was destroyed. [The city, if it is a city, represented by the symbol, Babylon, is not known definitively. Babylon represents everything that is evil, such as, Satan, demons, Antichrist, False Prophet, false religions, non-repentant sinners.] Every island and mountain destroyed. Great hailstones fell from heaven. Men did not repent but kept on blaspheming God. (Rev. 16:17-21).

Chapter 17
Vision 6
a bowl angel spoke.

great harlot who sits on waters = false religions of the world.

fornication = idolatry

scarlet beast = Antichrist

false church (religion)

—idolatry
—inhabitants
—lies

false religion

Antichrist
—7 heads = 7 whole world
—10 horns = 10 kings or rulers that the Antichrist controls

Antichrist
—ascend out of hell
—perdition = complete ruin

the 'bowl' angel spoke

Chapter 17
Vision 6
one of the seven angels who had the seven bowls, came and talked with me (John), saying to me, "Come, I will show you the judgment of the great harlot who sits on many waters, with whom the kings of the earth committed fornication, and the inhabitants of the earth were made drunk with the wine of her fornication." (Rev. 17:1—2)

woman sitting on a scarlet beast which was full of names of blasphemy, having seven heads and ten horns. (Rev. 17:3)

scarlet woman, the great harlot, Babylon the great, mother of harlots (Rev. 17:5)
—fornication with harlot
—idolaters
—wine of her fornication

Babylon, the great city or community which reigns over the kings of the earth (17:5)

the beast that carries her (the scarlet woman) has seven heads and ten horns (17:3 & 7)

the beast that you saw was, and is not and will ascend out of the bottomless pit and go to perdition (Rev. 17:8).

the angel said to me (John), "Why did you marvel? I will tell you the mystery of the woman and of the beast that carries her, which has

7 heads = 7 mountains =
whole earth.
7 kings = 7 empires of 7
world kingdoms.

5 kings (or empires) have
fallen.
They are: Egypt, Assyria,
Babylon, Mede-Persia,
and Greece.

1 empire is: Rome (in
John's day).

1 empire is yet to come,
which is the Revived
Roman Empire.
(See Daniel 2 & 9:27)

[See Daniel 7 and 8 for
the definition of beast
and horn.]

the seven heads and the ten horns. The beast that you saw was,
and is not, and will ascend out of the bottomless pit and go to
perdition. And those who dwell on the earth will marvel, whose names
are not written in the Book of Life from the foundation of the world,
when they see the beast that was, and is not, and yet is. (17:7-8)
Here is the mind which has wisdom: The seven heads are seven
mountains on which the woman sits on. There are also seven kings.
Five have fallen, one is, and the other has not yet come. And when
he comes, he must continue a short time. And the beast that was,
and is not, is himself also the eighth, and is of the seven, and is
going to perdition. And the ten horns which you saw are ten kings
who have received no kingdom as yet, but they receive authority for
one hour as kings with the beast. These are of one mind, and they will
give their power and authority to the beast. These will make war with
the Lamb, and the Lamb will overcome them, for He is <u>Lord of lords</u>
and King of kings; and those who are with Him are called, chosen,
and faithful." And he said to me, "The waters which you saw, where
the harlot sits, are peoples, multitudes, nations, and tongues. And
the ten horns which you saw on the beast, these will hate the harlot,
make her desolate and naked, eat the flesh and burn her with fire.
For God has put it into their hearts to fulfill His purpose, to be of one
mind, and to give their kingdom to the beast, until the words of God
are fulfilled. And the woman whom you saw is that great city which
reigns over the kings of the earth." (17:9-18)

Chapter 18
Vision 7
angel spoke

Chapter 18
Vision 7
another angel coming down from heaven, having great authority, and
the earth was illuminated with his glory. And he cried mightily with a
loud voice, saying, "Babylon the great is fallen, is fallen, and has
become a habitation of demons, a prison for every foul spirit, and a
cage for every unclean and hated bird! For all the nations have drunk
of the wine of the wrath of her fornication, the kings of the earth have
committed fornication with her, and the merchants of the earth have
become rich through the abundance of her luxury." (Rev. 18:1-3)

another voice from
heaven

another voice from heaven saying, "Come out of her, my people, lest
you share in her sins, and lest you receive of her plagues. For her sins
have reached to heaven, and God has remembered her iniquities.
Render to her just as she rendered to you, and repay her double
according to her works in the cup which she has mixed, mix for her
double. In the measure that she glorified herself and lived luxuriously,
in the same measure give her torment and sorrow; for she says in her
heart, 'I sit as queen, and am no widow, and will not see sorrow.'
Therefore her plagues will come in one day—death and mourning and
famine. And she will be utterly burned with fire, for strong is the Lord
God who judges her."

"And the kings of the earth who committed fornication and lived luxuriously with her will weep and lament for her, when they see the smoke of her burning, standing at a distance for fear of her torment, saying, 'Alas, alas, that great city Babylon, that mighty city! For in one hour your judgment has come.' And the merchants of the earth will weep and mourn over her, for no one buys their merchandise anymore: merchandise of gold and silver, precious stones and pearls, fine linen and purple, silk and scarlet, every kind of citron wood, every kind of object of ivory, every kind of object of most precious wood, bronze, iron, and marble: cinnamon and incense, fragrant oil and frankincense, wine and oil, fine flour and wheat, cattle and sheep, horses and chariots, and bodies and souls of men. And the fruit that your soul longed for has gone from you, and you shall find them no more at all. The merchants of these things, who became rich by her, will stand at a distance for fear of her torment, weeping and wailing, and saying, 'Alas, alas, that great city that was clothed in fine linen, purple, and scarlet, and adorned with gold and precious stones and pearls! For in one hour such great riches came to nothing.' And every shipmaster, all who travel by ship, sailors, and as many as trade on the sea, stood at a distance and cried out when they saw the smoke of her burning, saying, 'What is like this great city?' And they threw dust on their heads and cried out, weeping and wailing, and saying, 'Alas, alas, that great city, in which all who had ships on the sea became rich by her wealth! For in one hour she is made desolate. ' Rejoice over her, O heaven, and you holy apostles and prophets, for God has avenged you on her!"(Rev. 18:9-20)

mighty angel

a mighty angel took up a stone like a great millstone and threw it into the sea, saying, "Thus with violence the great city Babylon shall be thrown down, and shall not be found anymore. The sound of harpists, musicians, flutists, and trumpeters shall not be heard in you anymore. And no craftsman of any craft shall be found in you anymore. And the sound of a millstone shall not be heard in you anymore. And the light of a lamp shall not shine in you anymore. And the voice of bridegroom and bride shall not be heard in you anymore. For your merchants were the great men of the earth, for by your sorcery all the nations were deceived. And in her was found the blood of prophets and saints, and of all who were slain on the earth." (18:21-24)

Chapter 19
Christ's 2nd Coming
multitude in heaven

Chapter 19
Christ's <u>2nd Coming</u>
a loud voice of a great multitude in heaven, saying, "Alleluia! Salvation and glory and honor and power to the Lord our God! For true and righteous are His judgments, because He has judged the great harlot who corrupted the earth with her fornication; and He has avenged on her the blood of His servants shed by her." Again they said, Alleluia! And her smoke rises up forever and ever." (19:1-3)

24 elders and 4 creatures	saying, "Amen, Alleluia!" (Rev. 19:4)
voice from throne (Jesus Christ)	saying, "Praise our God, all you His servants and those who fear Him, both small and great!" (Rev. 19:5).
voice of a great multitude	the voice of a great multitude, as the sound of many waters and as the sound of mighty thunderings, saying, "Alleluia! For the Lord God Omnipotent reigns! Let us be glad and rejoice and hive Him glory, for the marriage of the Lamb has come, and His wife has made herself ready." Then he said to me (John), "Write: 'Blessed are those who are called to the marriage supper of the Lamb!'" And he said to me, "These are the true sayings of God." And I fell at his feet to worship him. But he said to me "See that you do not do that! I am your fellow servant, and of your brethren who have the testimony of Jesus. Worship God! For the testimony of Jesus is the spirit of prophecy." (19:6-10)
Lamb's bride = the Christian church	
Jesus Christ —eyes —on His head —name . —name —robe —mouth —rule —name	Faithful and True (Rev. 19:11) —like a flame of fire —many crowns —no one knows but Himself —Word of God —dipped in blood —sharp sword —rod of iron —King of kings and Lord of lords
angel in the sun	an angel standing in the sun; and he cried with a loud voice, saying to all the birds that fly in the midst of heaven, "Come and gather together for the supper of our great God, that you may eat the flesh of kings, the flesh of captains, the flesh of mighty men, the flesh of horses and of those who sit on them, and the flesh of all people, free and slave, both small and great." (Rev. 19:17-18).

Chapter 20:1-10
Christ's Millennial Reign

Chapter 20:1-10
The devil is bound and cast into hell for 1000 years so that he can not deceive the nations. Saints reign with Christ for 1000 years. After 1000 years Satan is released. He deceives many from all over the world to follow him. Satan battles God in the great Gog and Magog war. God defeats Satan and his followers. God throws Satan into the lake of fire where the Antichrist and False Prophet are. (Rev. 20:1-10).

Chapter 20:11-15
God's Judgment Day

Chapter 20:11-15
God judges all people of the world. The Book of Life was opened to see if Jesus Christ has your name in it, or if it has been blotted out. If it is blotted out other books are opened to see if you had sinned.

	[All men are sinners (Rom. 3:23) and God will by no means clear the guilty (Ex. 34:7).] Anyone not found written in the Book of Life will be cast into the lake of fire. Death and Hades are also cast into the lake of fire. (Rev. 20:11-15).
<u>**Chapters 21 and 22**</u> **Eternity Described**	**Chapters 21 and 22** God creates a new heaven and a new earth. It will last forever. There is no death, nor sorrow, nor crying, nor any pain. There is no darkness and no need for a sun, nor a moon, nor any stars because Jesus Christ supplies the new world its light. (Rev. 21 and 22). Amen, Amen.

CHAPTER 17

CONCLUSIONS

The rapture of all Christians is going to happen very, very soon; probably in the year 2022.

If my calculation is correct, the end of this age and the start of the next age—the millennial age—will begin in 2029. The seven year gap between 2022 and 2029 is also referred to as the seventieth week of Daniel mentioned in Dan. 9:24-27. This period is also called the tribulation period spoken of in Revelation; Chapter 4 through Chapter 19.

The tribulation period discussed in the book of Revelation occurs during this time. It is called the Lord's Day and the start of the seventh millennium or Christ's Millennial Reign. Seven years earlier, or 2022, the rapture will occur. This is the end of this age, which is what the Catholics, the Lutherans and other amillennialists believe.

In short:

0-6000 years = Man's Days or six millenniums of history.

The rapture as described in I Thess. 4:13-18 will occur in 2022.

The tribulation period is seven years in duration and the signing of the covenant between the Antichrist and the nation of Israel. Also Dan. 9:24-27.

2029 = the start of the seventh millennium which is also the start of the millennial reign of Jesus Christ.

Dear Reader,

The author would like to hear your thoughts and comments about this book.

His U. S. postal address is: 3735 S. 268th St., Kent, WA. 98032.
His e-mail address is: darrellgenzlinger@gmail.com.
His telephone number is: 253-852-6597.

NOTES AND COMMENTS